THE BABY

Whisperer

alison –
Honorary
Baby Whisperer!!
George

GEORGE POPE

iUniverse®

THE BABY WHISPERER

iUniverse books may be ordered through booksellers or by contacting:

iUniverse
1663 Liberty Drive
Bloomington, IN 47403
www.iuniverse.com
844-349-9409

Because of the dynamic nature of the Internet, any web addresses or links contained in this book may have changed since publication and may no longer be valid. The views expressed in this work are solely those of the author and do not necessarily reflect the views of the publisher, and the publisher hereby disclaims any responsibility for them.

Any people depicted in stock imagery provided by Getty Images are models, and such images are being used for illustrative purposes only.
Certain stock imagery © Getty Images.

ISBN: 978-1-6632-2858-1 (sc)
ISBN: 978-1-6632-2859-8 (e)

Library of Congress Control Number: 2021918184

Print information available on the last page.

iUniverse rev. date: 09/07/2021

CONTENTS

DEDICATION

I wish I could dedicate this book, by name, to all the health care providers and volunteers I have worked with at the Children's Hospital. But that would make the dedication longer than the book itself. And even then, I know I would leave out many who should be included.

So, this book is dedicated to the Children's Hospital doctors, nurses, therapists, and all those who directly support them.

They are the most caring, the most compassionate, and by far, the most competent group of professionals I have ever been associated with.

CHAPTER 1

Introduction

I recently dropped by our local library to see if anything new was on the shelf. Discovering a new spy thriller, I proceeded to check-out where I waited behind a mom who was with two kids in a two-baby stroller. One, maybe fours old, was totally engrossed in his book; the other, perhaps a one-year-old, was loudly letting everyone know she was ready for lunch and a nap.

Finally, Mom turned with an armload of books. She noticed me.

"Oh my God! George! Look! It's Mal!" She pointed to the little boy. "You held him in the NICU. Look how big he is!"

This exclamation, in the staid library, drew a crowd. Three librarians and several patrons drifted over to check out the commotion. Mom, who I recognized but couldn't pull up a name, continued.

"Mal came early and had to go into the NICU. George was there to hold him when we couldn't be there." She took a breath. "Even when I was there, whenever Mal heard George's voice, he would perk up. They were best friends forever."

Clara! I remembered her story of how her water broke in the middle of a baby shower and the ensuing pandemonium that would forever redefine the term pandemonium.

All eyes tuned to me. A man said, "Guys don't hold babies. That's what women do."

"Look," I replied with one of my two standard responses, "if I'm in the hospital and nobody visits me, it's probably what I deserve. But a baby does not deserve that." Several nods; some began to drift away.

"Parents should be there," a woman muttered under her breath.

Since that is one of the most frequent comments I get, I responded. "There are lots of legitimate reasons parents can't be there as much as they want. I'm there to hold their babies when they can't be there."

"I've always wanted to do that," a second women said which allowed me to pass out hospital information cards I always have on hand.

The one-year-old clearly let it be known she was ready to leave. The gathering dispersed. Another day in the life of a Baby Whisperer.

Before I continue, four notes:

1. Unless specifically noted otherwise, all references to the 'Children's Hospital', or 'the hospital' refer to the Medical University of South Carolina (MUSC) Shawn Jenkins Children's Hospital in Charleston, SC, which provides the most advanced pediatric care possible in more than 26 specialty areas. U.S. News & World Report (USNW) consistently ranks the MUSC Shawn Jenkins Children's Hospital as one of the best in the U.S. My primary goal with this book is to raise funds for this hospital. Yes, I will reimburse myself for out-of-pocket expenses; all else will be donated back to the Intensive Care and Oncology Units to help reimburse their medical teams' out-of-pocket expenses.

2. In this book, in order to strictly protect the privacy of patients, family, and medical staff, I use fictitious names. In some cases, I combine stories or switch genders. Every baby picture herein was taken by a mom who gave it to me with written permission to use in this book.

3. And as I note throughout, as a volunteer, I am only told what I need to know concerning a baby's medical condition. Any medical comments herein on my part were found on open sourced information on the internet.

4. My secondary goal in this book is to share heart-warming, uplifting, and sometimes downright amusing stories I have experienced in my sixteen years holding babies. Still, we are talking about the Intensive Care Units of a children's hospital where, by definition, one finds the sickest and the most fragile children and babies. Most, I am happy to report, do move on into hopefully productive and happy lives. But some don't.

I include these stories as well.

CHAPTER 2

What is a Baby Whisperer?

I suppose most people remember the Robert Redford movie, *The Horse Whisperer* from the 1980s, and the later TV show, *The Dog Whisperer*. Both were about a human who somehow was able to make a connection with, work with, and calm an animal that was basically out-of-control.

I, a Baby Whisperer, for reasons unknown, seem to have the ability to connect with and comfort the smallest of humans. It is a gift I didn't discover until I was sixty-five years old. I wish I had found it earlier, but I have now come to accept that 'for everything there is a season'.

For the past sixteen years, at least twice a week, I go to the Children's Hospital in Charleston, SC to hold and comfort babies. A definition of success for me is if the baby I am holding totally relaxes and drifts into a deep sleep.

For the first few years I volunteered in the Oncology Unit. In the last ten years, or so, my first stop has been the Neonatal Intensive Care Unit (NICU) which is for babies under twenty-eight days old. Other units I have served in over the years have included the Pediatric Intensive Care Unit (PICU) for children up to eighteen years old, the Pediatric Cardiac Intensive Unit (PCICU), and the Infant and Toddler's Unit.

The Intensive Care Units, also called Critical Care Units, are a non-stop twenty-four hour a day, seven-days a week hospital activity. At any given time, day or night, holidays and weekends, anxious parents hover, alarms beep, babies fret and cry, ventilators huff and puff, highly sensitive machine circuits cut out, x-rays and sonograms are being taken, and bedside evaluations, consultations, and procedures are underway while doctors, nurses, therapists, medical/nursing students, and technicians, always busy, and almost always seemingly behind schedule, scurry about.

The term Critical Care Units has come into being with the new Children's Hospital, which opened in March 2020. Whereas the Intensive Care Units in the old hospital, one for babies under twenty-eight days old, a second for children up to eighteen years old, and a third unit for cardiac cases, were located on several floors in two different building—a function of necessary expansion into available space as workloads grew—each unit in the new hospital is consolidated on one floor. In this book, I will usually refer to them as Intensive Care as that is still the term used by most medical staff.

Most Intensive Care Unit staff say they work in the hardest units in the hospital with the sickest and most fragile patients. They fight to keep the 24-weeker alive, to save babies born with damaged or non-cooperating body organs, and to comfort babies born addicted to opioids, heroin, and cocaine. They fight every single day and night for these miracle babies and children, both for the families and for themselves. Working in intensive care can be heart wrenching, inspiring, and rewarding. Each day is a new adventure and a new struggle.

This is not something I ever dreamed I would do, but some sixteen years ago, a friend literally grabbed me by the ear and marched me to the hospital volunteer office—more on that later—and the rest is history.

Where do I fit in?

I am a Baby Whisperer.

This is my story.

CHAPTER 3

Long Haul Story: Cover-boy Luke

During my time in the NICU, I often hold an individual baby no more than one or two times. This is because of a number of reasons: parent(s) may be present (Yay!), the baby may have gone home (Yay!), a nurse or therapist may be working with the baby ("Come back later if you can't find another baby."), or the baby I had held only a few days ago may not be 'holdable' for any number of medical reasons (Remember, this is the NICU). My stories of holding these short-term babies will, mostly, be included in various stories throughout the book.

There are times, however, when I meet up with a baby who will become my best friend forever for weeks or sometimes months. If parents are around, I get to know them as well as the doctors, nurses, therapists, social workers, and other medical team support staff who are working with that baby. These are my Long-Haul Babies, and I will intersperse their stories throughout the book as separate chapters.

I, once again, note that baby pictures in this book were taken by Mom, who either gave or sent them to me as we became close. And I do have written permission from each mom to use these pictures in this book.

My first Long Haul baby story is about Luke, my cover-boy. I never knew details about Luke's medical situation. All I knew was that when we were together, he was totally happy, content, and relaxed. Doctors, nurses, therapists, technicians, and even Mom, who I got to know, would come into the room and smile when they saw how happy and peaceful Luke was.

There were even times when Luke's Mom would come in and when I would suggest she hold Luke, she would decline. "I don't want to change a thing. He is so content with you."

Virtually every person who knew I was writing this book and who had seen the picture of George and Luke said, "That has got be your cover."

When I asked, Luke's Mom's response was, "By all means YES! We would be so honored for you to use the picture with Luke!"

It was with Luke when I first began to wonder if everyone in this life with whom I have become best friends tended to immediately fall asleep when I started talking and storytelling. Life's mysteries continue to unfold.

Luke's other best friend forever in the NICU was Nurse Maddie, who by chance, suggestion, or special request always seemed to be with Luke when I was volunteering. It was Maddie who told me that Luke was totally partial to his Dad and to me.

"We guys have to stick together," I commented.

When I mentioned this to Mom, she laughed and said, "Anyone can see that. I'm happy when Luke is happy."

Nurses have the biggest hearts!

CHAPTER 4

Brief Bio

I believe to understand my story, you will need to know just a bit about me.

I grew up in very small-town Mississippi. How small? My high school graduating class numbered seventeen. With few expectations, I went to Mississippi State University—Hail State! Turns out I loved history and actually completed my master's degree thinking I would pursue a Ph.D. and be an academic historian.

So much for thinking ahead. Instead, I joined the Peace Corps and spent two very pleasant, and as it turned out, life changing years in Chile. Returning home in the mid-1960s hoping for an international career, I took a job where I worked on international agricultural issues, including trade negotiations, marketing, international production statistics, and the operational aspects of food aid. The selling point for me was that the agency I worked for had offices in some sixty U.S. embassies around the world.

It was a great thirty-year career. I spent approximately half of my career in Washington, where I worked on the food aid component of international disaster relief programs. In Washington, I also learned that I was born to be a bureaucrat, which was not something I ever dreamed but which worked well for me. For reasons I never really understood, I almost always managed to be at the right place at the right time, and just as important, to be long gone when dreams, schemes, and careers collapsed.

Note: I believe this ability to not only survive, but to thrive, in a bureaucracy has been a benefit even in the NICU where I, a volunteer, am at the absolute bottom of the bureaucratic ladder. I know my place, my role, and I am totally comfortable with the bureaucratic swirl going on around me as I sit, hold, and comfort those babies.

Our family, my wife Lucretia and our daughters Elizabeth and Susan, was posted to six US embassies—Lagos, Jakarta, Seoul, Paris, Brussels, and Tokyo.

Folks sometimes ask—Lagos? Well, you have to start somewhere. I enjoyed Nigeria even though I admit there were WAWA (West Africa Wins Again) instances when a bit less excitement would have been appreciated. Almost everyone who has worked or lived in West Africa has WAWA stories. Mine will have to wait for another book.

Overall, we traveled, met, and worked with incredibly wonderful and interesting people on incredibly interesting issues. We learned about foreign countries, cultures, and languages.

Speaking of languages, some of my embassy language gaffs are still cited as cautionary tales. A former Korean colleague still reminds me of the time thirty years ago when I 'insulted' a high-level Korean official's grandmother by using the wrong tense when asking that official about his upcoming trip to US.

By the mid 1990s, it was clear it was time to slow down and figure out where we would retire. My suggestion that we retire to Mississippi got absolutely nowhere.

In the spring of 1997, Lucretia came back from Brussels, found the perfect building lot in a golf course community just north of Charleston, and supervised the design and construction of our new house. We moved in and began our low country life early in 1998.

CHAPTER 5

Retirement: A Different Ball Game

The biggest thing I had to get used to in retirement was that it was the first time since kindergarten I didn't have to get up, go somewhere, and do something someone else had decided for me. The first few weeks were great, but soon the "WHAT NOW?" question loomed.

I quickly realized how lucky I was that I did have skills that former associates, both in and out of government, were happy to use on a consulting basis. I was able to do work I enjoyed with folks I liked without having to do the 'stuff' involved will full time employment—sorting-out confusing and contradictory bureaucratic pronouncements, unraveling personnel issues, sitting through endless meetings leading nowhere, and surviving bond drives and combined giving campaigns.

I actually made a trip back to Nigeria where I accompanied a U.S. trade team. I was the expert on Nigeria who was helping the team members find new markets for their products. Naturally, WAWA struck in full force. Our Nigerian host had convinced our team leader it would be much cheaper and more convenient to charter an airplane to hop around the country instead of depending on notoriously unpredictable domestic airlines. Unfortunately, no one checked the credit worthiness of the recommended charter airline. The team found ourselves stranded in a remote Nigerian airport about as far from anywhere as one could be. The airline's credit was non-existent and nobody was going anywhere until cash hit the table. After a couple of hours of finger pointing, shouting, and threats, all thirty or so members of the team had to pull out credit cards so we could gas-up and continue our tour. I don't think it was rated as one of the great trade team success stories.

Overall, I was comfortably busy with consulting while learning about the low country, making new friends, finding a new church, and playing tennis and golf. But by mid-decade 2000, my consulting opportunities dwindled to a precious few, and I realized it was time to start seriously looking for volunteer opportunities.

I volunteered at a national forest helping visitors map out trails, pinpoint bathroom locations, and explaining to visitors that taking up-close photos of kids and alligators was not a good idea. Later, I took and helped serve meals at local homeless shelters where I learned everybody has a truly heartbreaking story, some of which are actually true.

Then, in 2005, I discovered the Children's Hospital. If I had listed five hundred things I might do in retirement, volunteering in a children's hospital would not have even been considered. But a friend kept nagging: "You should be holding those babies." Finally, to get her off my back, I gave it a try. I now know it was a "God thing".

CHAPTER 6

Wait a Minute! Did You Just Mention God?

Yes! But not to worry. While my story does have spiritual aspects, this is not that kind of book.

First, a word from my fan club, which at the moment totals one member, my wife Lucretia, who has signed-up on a trial basis. She is convinced I love going to the children's hospital because I am on the same emotional and intellectual level as the babies I hold.

My rebuttal is that when I am holding a baby and start to tell a story or sing a song, the baby can't get up and walk out of the room like she does.

Lucretia also says I am far more spiritual than institutionally religious. I have no argument with her analysis.

Oh, by the way, I have had two conversations with my Creator, who in this story, I will call God.

Now, before you say, "Burn the book! This guy's a nut case," hear me out.

The first conversation came many years ago, but I remember it as if it had occurred just now. It was early fall in the DC area but the daylight savings time change had not yet occurred. I had gotten home, had supper, and was walking the back yard trying to figure out how many leaf bags I would need for the upcoming weekend's leaf rake.

13

I'm not sure why, but I picked up a leaf and held it to the setting sun. I was immediately taken by the incredible intricacy of the leaf's structure. Every vein seemed to perfectly flow into a smaller vein until they were too small to see. I marveled at the perfection and then heard a voice. I first thought someone was standing beside me, but I was alone.

The conversation went like this:

Voice: "So, you're impressed with the perfection of the leaf?"

Me: "What, what, what?"

Voice: "Look around you. I could tell you exactly how many more there are within your sight. Each leaf is exactly how I want it to be."

Me: "What, what, what?"

Voice: "For me, leaves are just a throwaway."

Me, finally catching on: "Throwaway? They're perfect."

Voice: "Exactly! George," (Note we are now on a first name basis) "if I can do this with leaves, do you doubt my ability to do anything?"

Me, now totally awed: "Absolutely not."

Voice: "Good! Keep that in mind."

And that was that, except at that moment I was totally hooked and to this day, maybe fifty years later, that conversation remains as clear as if it had just happened. And while I have strayed—boy, have I ever strayed—I have never doubted for a second that God has been sitting on my shoulder keeping an eye on me, or more likely, rolling His or Her eyes at the incredibly dumb things I continually do.

And, yes, there was a second conversation, which I will get to later.

Finally, just to clear the air, I do have a ritual I follow whenever I first hold a baby. Quietly, very quietly, as religion is a very sensitive issue in the hospital, once the baby and I are settled, I begin a very quiet one-way conversation. I always use the baby's first name as I am convinced even the smallest baby knows its name. I am also convinced that even the smallest baby knows when they are being talked to as opposed to when medical staff are standing round talking about them. When I am not sure of the baby's first name, it will either be 'little brother' or 'little sister', as in "Okay, little brother, let's you and me get to know each other."

Anyway, the conversation goes like this: "Okay, little brother, or baby's name, it's you, it's me, and I am inviting God to join our little party right here and right now."

I'll pause a few seconds, then continue. "I am asking God to flood this room and this entire unit with love and peace." I do not ask for healing as I am convinced that God knows exactly what is going to happen and doesn't need me reminding what I think should be happening.

At this point, I sit quietly and wait.

And yes, I do feel God's love pouring in, maybe through me into the baby, maybe through the baby into me. How cool is that?

Most times, but not always, I can feel the baby starting to unwind. Clenched fists loosen, knotted shoulder muscles relax, and frantic eyes that had been darting around seeking an escape route begin to get heavy.

Usually, but not always, within ten minutes, the baby who has come to me totally terrified is completely at peace. And yes, I totally sense these babies are terrified. Here they are, just born, hooked up to who knows how many machines, monitors, and tubes. Often, their only contact with other humans is when someone comes by and sticks, pricks, or shoves a tube up their nose, or when a group of strangers stand around talking about them, not to them.

Before you say, "Sure, sure! Nice happy talk. But you're dreaming. No way! No way! Simply holding and talking to a baby can't produce those results," there have been, to me at least, real world confirmations.

Sometimes, not often but maybe three times every couple of years, I get a confirmation that something special has indeed taken place.

In the NICU, as I sit and hold babies, there is an unending stream of doctors, nurses, and therapists passing by. Over time, I have noticed they, probably unaware they are doing so, automatically glance at the monitors the baby is hooked up to as they stride by. These are the monitors you see on all TV hospital shows beeping away as they track second-by-second heart beats, respiration levels, levels of oxygen in the blood steam, and other vital indicators.

So, these doctors, nurses, and therapists pass by on their way to somewhere else, glance at the monitor, and continue on. But as I say, maybe three times every couple of years, one will get a couple of steps past George and the baby, stop, turn around, come back, look at the monitor, look at the baby, look at the monitor again, then say something, almost to themselves, like, "That's the most peaceful that baby has been," or "Those are the best numbers we've seen." Then they look at me and say, "Thank you!" Then they turn and are off to wherever.

I have never gotten any award, any promotion, or even any other compliment that means as much to me as simply knowing in some small way I have helped this child. It is why I will come back until I can't.

Recently, there was another confirmation that something special has happened. In the new Children's Hospital, there is what I call 'The Twins Corridor' where rooms are larger than elsewhere so NICU twins or triplets, mostly early-arrivers, can be together. This makes it more convenient, both for medical staff and for when parents visit.

But this time there was a slight change as the two babies in this room were siblings of a twin who had already gone home. On this day, I had barely entered the Twins Corridor when nurses started pointing me towards that room. When I stuck my head in the door, there was no question which baby needed holding. One was sound asleep, the other was in full fury letting everyone within earshot know, "I gotta get out of this place if it's the last thing I ever do" (slight adaptation on the 1960s rock-song about Vietnam). This little guy's angry was the absolute definition of angry.

So, with the nurse's help, this little guy and I settled in. I started rocking, singing, and talking. Sure enough, slowly but surely, the baby began to calm down and within in a few minutes, was sound asleep. Whew! The other baby in the room was already in dreamland.

A half hour later, the mom of the other baby arrived and once she was settled, we began to chat. I had noticed her baby's name was very Irish and made a comment about the heritage.

She laughed: "Actually, we aren't Irish. When I found out I was pregnant, my due-date was St. Patrick's Day, so my husband and I decided on two really Irish names. Then, when the boys came early, we agreed to stick with the Irish names. It will give us something to talk about when they grow up."

At that point, she did a double-take and said, "I just realized this is the first time I've been here when he," she nodded towards the sleeping Baby I was holding, "wasn't really unhappy about something."

CHAPTER 7

A Difficult Beginning: Guess Who Comes to the Rescue?

It took just a couple of shifts for me to realize volunteering at the hospital was what I was born to do.

Today, over sixteen years later, I have developed several responses whenever people ask, "Why are you holding babies? That's what women do. Guys don't hold babies." As mentioned in the introduction, one response is "Look, if I'm in the hospital and nobody visits me, it's probably just what I deserve. But a little baby has done nothing to deserve being alone in the hospital."

But when I think it is appropriate and won't result in a punch in the nose or simply being fired, I say, "It is the only place I see miracles happen."

That response led to my second conversation with God.

In those early days, I was having a hard time accepting the concept of sick babies. The more I dithered, the more upset I became. Then I started having angry one-way conversations—rants might be a better term—with God. "What have these babies done to deserve this? And I won't accept it is because this baby's great-great-uncle did something that made you unhappy and this is your pay-back. No way!" As I noted, this was a one-way conversation.

Then, one day, there was a reckoning. I was alone in a room holding a baby who was absolutely, positively the unhappiest and the most fretful creature on this earth. I was in the middle of an internal rant— "Okay, God, what's going on here? This baby doesn't deserve this. Don't you even come across to me with this loving God business. This isn't right!"

Just at the point where I was going to call the nurse, hand the baby back, and walk out of that place forever, once again, a conversation.

And once again it was George and an empty room, except for the baby. But this time, I had no doubt who was talking.

God: "George! You are exactly where I want you to be."

Me (my now standard refrain): "What, what, what?"

God: "You are exactly where I want you to be."

Me: "What, what, what?"

God: "You are here to show these babies my love. Can you do that?"

Me, finally getting the message: "Yes. I can do that."

God: "You show my love and leave the rest, which is not for you to understand, to me. Is that clear?"

Me: "Yes."

God: "And I want you to show my love to everyone you meet in this hospital. Can you do that?"

Me: "I can do that."

God: "Good. Now quit whining. Call the nurse. This baby is ready to eat."

And that was that, except when I regained my composure— conversations with God can be quite disconcerting—I realized the baby was sound asleep and totally at peace.

I was hooked. Being me, I did dither for a while wondering why it took me sixty-five years to discover where I was supposed to be. Then I accepted that everything on this earth does indeed have its own time, its own reason, and its own season.

Since then, from the moment I walk into the hospital until the moment I depart, I try to speak to and smile at every person I meet. I have learned to spot people who are hopelessly lost in the hospital labyrinth and help them find their way to wherever.

Speaking of being hopelessly lost, every time a nurse asks me to take something somewhere or to go pick up something somewhere, I am hopelessly lost the second I walk out of the NICU. My only recourse is to 'depend on the kindness of strangers.' (My tribute to Tennessee Williams who grew up in my home town of Columbus, Mississippi.)

Continuing with the Baby Whisperer story, a particular challenge is to help people I find wandering around a parking garage who can't find their car. They either don't remember which floor they parked on, or which of the several hospital garages they parked in. I have learned it is best to take them to the security desk, who are experts in handling this type of situation. For lost cars, an attendant with a golf cart can drive them around until they spot their car.

Sometimes, in the panicked rush to get a child into the emergency room, a car will be left running. This is not as uncommon as one might think. In such instances, an attendant will park the car and take the keys to the security desk, who will wait for someone like me to show up so they can give them the keys and a parking ticket, sometimes already stamped with one day's fee, and a note as to where the car is parked. One less thing for panicked parents to worry about.

Once in the hospital, I make sure to greet every doctor, nurse, therapist, medical technician, every clerk, and especially, the staff who clean the bathrooms and mop the floors. I have learned that they, normally the silent troops, have huge hearts for the babies and parents, so I encourage them to consider volunteering when they retire.

And to wrap up religion, a story of how best intentions…

A few years ago, a retired nurse organized a group of ladies in her church to volunteer to hold babies. They were fantastic! Then one day and a couple of times later when I was volunteering, I noticed none of that group was around. I asked my Volunteer Coordinator what was going on.

"It was a disaster!" she moaned. "All of a sudden, we realized they were cornering people in the hallways, in elevators, in the snack bars, and even in a baby's room demanding to know if they knew Jesus. It was awful! I called them in and explained we were at risk of losing millions of dollars in federal grants. It was something we could not allow." She paused and took a breath. "They wouldn't budge, said it was something they were called to do. All I could do was say they couldn't do it here and ask them not to come back." Another pause. "I've had difficult conversations with volunteers who didn't work out, but I never, ever thought I would have to fire an entire group."

I should have let a bad situation lie. But no! George to the rescue! "I know these ladies," I said. "They make a huge contribution. Would you mind if I speak with them?"

The look I got should have warned me off, even when what I heard was, "You can try."

So, a couple of days later, I found myself facing a group of very upset ladies. "How about this approach?" I began. "Would you accept there are two types of ministry, a Tell Ministry where you tell people about your faith, and a Show Ministry where you show your faith?" This was an obvious play on the adage, 'Actions speak louder than words.' I continued, "If you can accept that and bring your Show Ministry to the hospital, you will be doing so much good for both the babies and their families."

I sat back, proud of myself for my brilliant solution.

To say I was handed my head on a platter would be a gross understatement. I hadn't been chewed-out like that since my first day of Army Basic Training where I learned the proper use of a tooth brush was to scrub a commode.

Even after thinking about this episode as I write this, I'm glad I tried because it was the babies who were the losers in this situation. Still, I hope if there is a next time, I will do a better job of reading between the lines when someone is trying to warn me off.

And it turned out there was a "rest of this story" which I will get to later in this book.

CHAPTER 8

Long Haul Baby Jake

Baby Jake was my first Long Haul Baby. We came together in late 2011. I remember the date since Baby Jake and my grandson Henry were born on the same day.

Like all Long-Haul Babies, Jake was born with serious medical issues. Remember, as a volunteer, I am only privy to information concerning a baby's medical condition that I need to know when holding that baby. However, since I often do become close to the family, they are often far less reticent in explaining their understanding of their baby's condition. And there are nurses and therapists who become close to the family as well. A couple I know still follow a special baby ten years after discharge.

As an aside, when I first became involved with the Pediatric Palliative Care Program, I was invited to sit in on their weekly staff meeting when they went over every baby's status and condition. After a couple of meetings, I disinvited myself. If they had been speaking Chinese, I would not have understood any less of the discussions. And anything I did understand was of no particular use when I was holding one of those babies, so, once again, I would file and forget.

Mom told me Jake had a necessary medical procedure in his future which experience had taught could not be done until a baby had reached a certain age and weight. The challenge was to keep Jake as safe and healthy as possible until he met those requirements. The major concern was infection, the scourge of the NICU.

Jake's mom was by his side from day one. We became fast friends while sharing stories of Jake and my grandson Henry. Jake's dad, who kept his job in the SC upstate, visited on weekends. Over time, I was accepted as Jakes's surrogate grandfather.

As with most babies in the NICU, getting Jake from where he was to where he needed to be so that the necessary procedure could take place was the challenge. I learned, not for the first time nor the last, that infections often had an insidious way of sneaking onto the scene. Seemingly, time after time, Jake would almost reach a point where the procedure could happen. Then an infection would appear and everything would-be put-on hold until the count-down process could start again. I can't remember a time I held Jake when I didn't have to go full precaution and wear both a surgical gown and gloves. A mask was not required, but this was pre-pandemic times.

Finally, Jake's condition and the procedure date coincided. The procedure was a complete success. Jake moved on to the getting ready to 'blow this joint' stage. Everybody was thrilled.

A couple of weeks after his procedure, I came to the NICU and learned Jake had been moved to the Infant and Toddlers Unit. He was almost ready to go home. I found a new NICU baby to hold, completed my shift, and went looking for Jake and Mom. In the Infant and Toddlers Unit, the door to Jake's room was closed, but the nurse said I could knock and go in, which I did. Mom, who was holding Jake, looked up and said, "My first time alone with my baby and who walks in but George Pope? It is exactly what I expected."

We chatted for a couple of minutes, but as I made ready to leave, she said, "I have a mountain of papers I have to get sorted-out, filled-out and signed. Could you hold him so I can find a room with a table so I can get started?"

So, for one last time, George and Jake were together to discuss the issues of this world and for the first time, watch sports on TV.

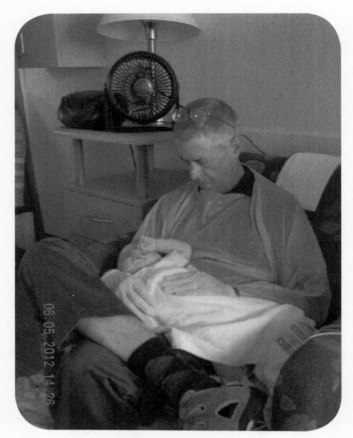

Baby Jake: Almost home

When Mom returned later, she took the above photo. Her comment when she gave me this photo almost ten years later was, "I remember snapping this photo after returning from an errand. You were both snoozing with some sports on the TV. It was so sweet and meant the world to me."

I, of course, totally dispute that I was snoozing. I was meditating. And it was interesting to me when I saw this picture that even when Jake was almost ready to go home, I was still in contact precaution gear. And a caution alert: If you are ever instructed to wear contact precaution gear, find a yellow gown. They 'breathe' whereas the blue ones don't.

And here is a picture of Jake, age nine. Smiles please!

Pick those berries, buddy!

CHAPTER 9

Volunteers

A George story on why we volunteer: As I was doing final edits on this book, I received an email from my daughter who is friends with the mother of a 3nd year Pediatric Resident. Her daughter had reported that recently during NICU rounds, there was a screaming baby who could not be calmed. The attending physician remarked, "Too bad we can't write a prescription for George Pope to come and hold this baby."

Children's Hospital volunteers do far more than hold babies. Of the approximate 190 Children's Hospital volunteers where I work, some 100 actually hold babies. The others do a variety of important jobs to support the hospital. One website—musckids.org—provides a full listing and explanation of volunteer opportunities. And my understanding is that Children's Hospitals around the country are always recruiting new volunteers. If you are interested, please don't wait to follow-up.

Factoid: I know far fewer volunteers than any other group of staff in the hospital. I am on a first name basis with more of the cleaning staff who come into the room to empty trash, scrub the bathroom, and mop the floor than I am with other volunteers. This is because as a volunteer, I come to the hospital, sign in, go to the NICU, hold a baby, and then go home. Over time, I get to know doctors, nurses, therapists, technicians, cleaning, and other medical support staff who come into the room where

I am with the baby. The other two or three volunteers on that NICU shift, who I may or may not know, are holding a baby somewhere else.

A few times a year, I help train new NICU volunteers who will shadow me on my shift. I introduce the new volunteer to staff. We take a tour of the NICU (special emphasis on restroom locations). I explain as best I can the machines and devices a baby may be connected to, and emphasize and re-emphasize the importance of infection control. Finally, we find a baby for the new volunteer to hold. I may or may not ever see that volunteer again.

Another interesting aspect of volunteering is that several full-time medical staff at the hospital also volunteer on their off-days and holidays. They will come to the Ronald McDonald House or other family support facilities on these emotionally charged special days to offer support to family members who have gathered.

Since this book is my story of volunteering, I will leave that discussion here.

Read on!

Pet Therapy

One of my favorite volunteer programs is pet therapy even though it is one about which I actually have few details. For example, what I had always thought as the Pet Therapy Program is now officially called the Therapy Animal Program. This is similar to what I later learned that what I had always though were Intensive Care Units are now officially known as Critical Care Units. Still, since everyone I know at the hospital still uses the term Intensive Care and Pet Therapy, those are the terms I will mostly use in this book.

Most of the pet therapy stories herein have been offered by those working directly in this program.

Pet Therapy has been a part of the Children's hospital for close to two decades. The majority of the time, it consisted of approximately three dozen therapy dogs and volunteer handlers coming into the main hospital to offer companionship and create a pleasant distraction to patients, family members and on occasion, medical care team members.

But by 2015, medical and veterinary scientists were realizing the therapeutic link between the humans and animals. Clinical studies showed that certified therapy dogs not only reduced stress, depression and blood pressure, they also improved self-esteem, increased physical mobility, provided comfort and eradicated loneliness. When partnered with physicians, therapists, and nurses, canine intervention can help patients reach health goals, remain positive, and stimulate motivation.

Today, some eighty Pet Therapy teams roam the halls of MUSC facilities with close to forty of those teams assigned to the Children's Hospital. Another dozen Pet Therapy Teams visit the many children's specialty clinics throughout the area.

These dogs specialize in tail wagging happiness:

– A little boy going through chemo was so self-conscious of his hair loss that his bubbling personality could not be found. In walked a therapy dog with a shaved hot spot on his hip. The little boy noticed and asks about it. The volunteer explained that shaving the hair was the dog's best defense against infection, and in time the hair would come back. Almost instantly, the little boy got out of bed and knelt down beside the dog and began to talk to him. "I know how you feel, but don't worry, we will both get better soon and we will both have our hair back!"

– The nurse was desperately trying to remove an IV from a little boy's hand. He was being discharged, but even the thought of going home was of no interest. He was terrified of having the needle pulled out from under his skin. Along comes a therapy dog, and the wagging tail caught his attention. The offer to walk the dog around the unit, if he let the nurse remove the IV needle, was so tempting he sat up straight, held onto the dog, squeezed his eyes tight and said, "Do it!" Anyone who saw those over-sized super hero pajamas strutting down the hallway swinging that leash will ever forget that moment.

- A high school piano prodigy refused to let her mom wheel her to the Atrium to practice. This all changed when she met the therapy dog of her dreams. She would cuddle with this dog for hours. When there was music softly playing in the room, the dog would snuggle on the bed and sleep till she snored. This inspired this little girl to practice whenever she could. She wanted to play for this dog she had grown to love. With a few phone calls, Animal Therapy staff were able to create a mini-concert in the main lobby area. When the wheelchair rolled into the lobby, volunteers, medical staff, family, and friends awaited. She played beautifully, and the dog shared her piano bench the entire time.

My personal Pet Therapy memory happened maybe fifteen years ago. I was in a unit where a group of residents, accompanied by an attending physician, were making rounds. The residents were grouped around the physician who was pointing out something on her note pad.

At that moment, a Pet Therapy volunteer with dog walked into the unit. The physician continued talking, then looked up to see… well, nobody.

The residents had all rushed to the dog and were kneeling and petting. I noted a flash of frustration, then a look of resignation from the physician, who then walked over to get her share of love. It wasn't long before it became a seemingly standard policy: Whenever a pet comes into the unit during rounds, there will be a two-minute break.

Stories like these are endless.

These dogs will ride gurneys into pre-op to help reduce the stress and anxiety a child feels before they are sedated and are often there when the child wakes up in post-op. They have made children speak for the first time due to trauma in their lives and have helped parents grieve over a terminal illness diagnosis or the loss of a child.

There is one unique aspect of pet therapy which I, the ultimate amateur, have come to realize is that the therapy animals clearly reflect the unending levels of extreme stress in the NICU. Doctors, nurses, medical-care staff, parents, and volunteers realize they are working in a critical care environment where a momentary focus lapse or even the most honest of mistakes could be disastrous. Somehow, adults are able to, at least outwardly, manage this never-ending stress.

The one stress outlet I have found is the often very black humor cartoons posted in staff restrooms and break rooms. I personally think they are amusing. But I have been advised, almost unanimously, not to include them in this book. So, dear readers, you will simply have to let your imagination run wild!

The two exceptions to not outwardly showing stress I have noted are young children who are visiting their sibling—somehow managing to get around strict prohibitions against such visits—and pet therapy dogs. Pet therapy dog owner after owner tell me their dog is good for, at most, ninety minutes before hitting the wall. One owner told me if they stay too long, her dog is so exhausted, she has to carry it to the car.

Therapy dogs can be found in MUSC pediatric rehabilitation centers and clinics all over the low country. Physical, recreational, occupational and even mental health clinics request and use MUSC Pet Therapy services to help children of all ages.

MUSC's numerous awards and high rankings have confirmed it is one of the most innovative and collaborative medical facilities in the country. This is apparent in the supportive ways they partner with the therapy animal program. I am told MUSC is one of the first, if not the first, hospital to provide an online Therapy Animal Story Time Library available to all patients twenty-four hours a day.

Pet Therapy is truly changing what's possible in health care one tail wag at a time.

And, a final therapy story--Music Therapy is another wonderful program. I love to sing along when a staff music therapist comes into the room where I am holding a baby, even though the therapist will often wince when I join in. "Daisy, Daisy, give me your answer true..." is my favorite. And when I am alone with a baby, I can spin "She'll be coming around the mountain when she comes" into an hour-long story-song. In my version, the baby's name replaces the 'she'. And everyone else in that song has a good time and a story to tell when 'she' comes 'round that mountain'.

In summary, the MUSC Volunteer program is active and growing. New volunteer orientation programs are organized several times a year. Interested? All you have do is call.

For more information on volunteer opportunities:

- muschealth.org/volunteer
- musckids.org (click on the 'ways to help' tab)

CHAPTER 10

Parents

Imagine for a very short moment what it must be like to be a parent, grandparent, or guardian whose child is in intensive care. When I first started volunteering, I would all too often see these folks, as alone as alone could be, in a state of shock and dismay while doctors, nurses, and therapists surrounded their child.

Personally, I can think of nothing more awful. So, I often will make a point of touring the unit when I first arrive simply to speak with parents. I will always introduce myself as a volunteer who is here to help out on any non-medical issue if I can.

Some parents are so engrossed in their child they clearly do not want to talk. I wish them well and move on. Others seem desperate for a conversation with someone who is not a medical figure. I have spent a three-hour shift holding a mom's hand while she told me her baby's history from the point of conception to the present moment, and then some.

And there are the seemingly oddball requests. I have heard variations on, "Where is the bathroom? I feel like I'm going to throw-up," or "If I don't pee now, I'm going to bust." Often people who made this comment are standing two feet away from a clearly marked restroom. I also get, "Where can I buy a tooth brush", "a washcloth", or whatever. Good news here: Small toiletry kits are now available for parents. And, there is always the "I have no idea where I parked the car."

With parents, I try to keep my mouth shut, my ears open, and simply listen. Still, there are those instances when I may find it appropriate to offer advice. Two deal with parent interaction with doctors. When parents make a frustration comment that they didn't understand something the doctor had said during rounds or consultations or they had forgotten to ask a question, I will suggest they keep a small notebook handy and write down their questions for medical staff. I point out that when doctors does come through, they are probably an hour behind schedule and in the hustle-bustle, and the parent may forget to ask a question. With the notebook handy, this problem is lessened.

And as a follow-up to the doctor's visit, when the parents look at each other and ask, "What did they say?" I suggest they ask the baby's nurse, who also sits in on rounds and consultations. Then keep asking until they are satisfied they understand what's going on with their baby.

The third occasion I might offer a suggestion is when the parents bring up religion. Once again, religion is a tricky, sensitive, and sometimes controversial issue in hospitals. This usually comes from parents who are not from the immediate area and takes the form of either, "We miss the support we get from our local church" or the more direct, "Are you churched?" (This is South Carolina!) or "Can you recommend a church around here?"

When this happens, I avoid the direct question, call the nurse over, and note that I think the parents would like to speak with a Hospital Chaplain. I do this because in today's environment, a chaplain must be invited to visit a patient. The days when ministers, pastors, or a chaplain could just drop-by are long past.

Once the nurse has confirmed my understanding, their response is almost always, "I'll make a call right now." We love our chaplains. They are so supportive."

When I do move on from visiting with parents, my default expression is, "This is the only place I tell people I hope I don't see them again, at least here in the hospital." Most parents smile at that.

One more example of why holding babies can be far more than just holding babies. One day, after I had put my baby back, I realized there was a very heated exchange going on around a baby two cribs away.

This was in the old hospital where most of the NICU was an open bay. The new hospital is different; most babies are in a single room. There are some doubles for twins, or when there is a need to double-up because there are more babies than available rooms. Guess what? There is a lively internal debate playing out on the inter-web on whether the open bay or private room is the better arrangement.

Open bay advocates point out that babies benefit from the social interaction the baby has with people walking by and that a nurse can pull their work station between the cribs. An NICU nurse seldom has more than two assigned babies, which would put the nurse no more than two steps away if something goes wrong with a baby.

The private room side argues that the open bay system deprives parents of privacy with their child. There are also discussions concerning if private rooms lessen the chance of infection.

My personal totally non-medical amateur view is if the objective is to get that baby out of the hospital as soon as possible, anything that helps achieve that goal should be adopted. I suspect this discussion will continue for some time.

Continuing with my story, two cribs away from where I had been holding another baby, a team of doctors and a chaplain were obviously trying to explain some upsetting news to very upset parents. The parents were having none of it and were seeking to place blame on whoever was responsible for their child's situation.

I then noted the chaplain, who I knew, was getting as upset as the parents. *Not good*, I thought. I walked up and tapped the chaplain on the shoulder. She wheeled around and for a moment I thought I was in line for a punch in the nose. Before she could say or do anything, I said, "Let's take a walk," and pulled her away. We had barely made it to the hallway when she looked at me and said, "Thanks, I'm okay now. I've got to get back in there." She turned and walked back into the unit.

I do not consider this a ministry. I am simply following instructions as best I can and hopefully using my gift.

The very good news is there is now a wonderful relatively new program, the Pediatric Palliative Care Program (PPCP) that directly addresses many of the issues mentioned above and more. It is the most important initiative I have seen in my sixteen years holding babies. In fact, one reason I am writing this book is to generate funds I will donate to the PPCP.

More on the PPCP later.

CHAPTER 11

Long Haul Story: Susie B

Parents play a huge role in every child's time in the hospital. Susie B's story is a good example. Susie B was a little girl maybe three years old when I first met her in the Infants and Toddlers Unit one Christmas Day as I was dropping off a plate of cookies for the lucky on-duty staff.

Susie B was sitting at the nurse's station. She was bright, she was perky, and she wanted more than one cookie. A spirited negotiation ensued. The nurses won. Susie B protested but finally selected her cookie. We all watched her totally enjoy it.

The next challenge was how to get her back to her room as she clearly was ready for a nap. Nurses to the rescue. A nurse pulled out one more present—I suspect several had brought presents to the Unit that day—and told Susie B she could open it in her room. Off they went.

I remember saying something about how cute Suzy B was and how I hoped her hospital stay would be short. The looks I received at this remark let me know all was not well. Finally, one nurse said, "She will be here a long time. You should make her your first stop whenever you are here." That was the extent of my official briefing.

What I learned over time was that Susie B had a condition that hopefully could be treated with a procedure. The problem was that experience had clearly shown the procedure could not be done until the child had reached a certain level of development. If the procedure were done any earlier, it would almost certainly fail and the child would be weaker than before.

Susie B was in a race against time which even to me she was losing. She would pick up an infection and be weaker than before when she recovered. A couple of times, she had to go to the Pediatric Intensive Care Unit (PICU). It was here when I learned another unwritten aspect of hospital etiquette. Once a patient is transferred from one unit to another, it is considered unacceptable and unprofessional for medical staff from the first unit to follow up, even to just stop by to say hello. I guess it is an out of sight, out of mind situation. The staff in the first Unit is expected to focus one hundred percent on patients under their direct care. And no matter how innocuous a just dropping-by visit might seem, the staff of the second unit might see it as an intrusion of how they were doing their job. In any event, it was a definite no-no.

But nurses are a resourceful lot. Soon I was hearing remarks along the lines of, "Susie B is your best friend forever. She would love it if you were with her." And of course, "Before you leave the hospital, you come back here and tell us what's going on." So, my shuttle mission began.

As if Susie's B's medical issues weren't enough, it was apparent that her parents were a negative multiplier. They were estranged. They simply could not be together. If they were in the hospital at the same time, a Jerry Springer TV show type brawl might erupt and bouncers would be needed to keep them apart. This is definitely something not in a nurse's hospital job description.

And then it became apparent that Dad had a substance abuse issue. Although he would loudly proclaim he had it beaten, it was clear it wasn't. To make matters worse, Dad struck-up another relationship in the hospital. To me, this was an unfolding story line even the writers of the trashiest soap opera would reject out of hand. But there it was and the unit staff had to figure out how to make the best of an awful situation, which they, as the absolute definition of professionals, did.

I am not sure if it was an established or informal schedule, but Mom and Dad would come to the hospital on different days. When they were not around each other, they would be fine with Susie B. The only time I would see Mom and Dad together was when the doctors needed a consultation. My sense was the doctors wanted to brief them together so there would be no accusations that they were telling one parent one thing and the other parent something different.

As all of this was going on, it was apparent even to me that Susie B was losing her race against time. I learned the doctors had considered, then dismissed, trying the procedure.

And yes, Susie B passed away.

But here, this story takes an unusual twist. Think back to Chapter 7 and my story about the church volunteer group pulled together by a retired nurse and how they were ultimately asked not to come back as they couldn't stop proselytizing every person they met in the hospital. In that story, I mentioned how I thought they were doing a wonderful job with the babies, and how I had spectacularly and unsuccessfully tried to persuade them to revise their approach and come back to the hospital.

My 'wonderful job' comment related to their work with Susie B. Those ladies loved that child, and she loved them in return. What I didn't know until the three nurses and I went to Susie B's funeral was the rest of the story.

My first clue dawned on me when I realized the funeral was taking place at the church where that volunteer group had let me know in no uncertain terms why they would not, could not, change their proselytizing approach. The second clue was when we saw Mom and Dad sitting peacefully together, supporting each other, in the front row of the church. And later at the reception, they seemed totally at ease with each other.

What I didn't know or realize until that moment was that the volunteer group had shown up at the hospital at exactly the right time and with the exact right message Mom and Dad needed to hear and were prepared to hear. And not only had that volunteer group adopted Susie B, they had, in effect, adopted Mom and Dad as well.

Coincidence? Maybe so, maybe not. But I had not put it all together until I began to think it through and write the Susie B Long Haul story.

Lesson learned, I hope: Never, ever assume you know everything there is to know about anything involving humans.

CHAPTER 12

Names

Question: Do you recognize the name Nevaeh? Read on!

One of my few regrets in volunteering is that in the beginning I did not have a small notebook in which I would list all the unusual names and the stories behind those names I have come across over the years.

I mentioned elsewhere that when I first arrive in the NICU, I will often walk the unit to say hello to parents and see if they wish to engage in conversation. One of the best conversation starters I have found is to ask about the baby's name. There always seems to be a story behind the name which the parents often want to share.

I'll ask the baby's name and whatever the parents say, I follow-up with, "I like that name. Is it a family name?"

As it turns out, all too often selecting a name is a long and sometimes heated family affair. There are always more family names to choose from than babies to name. And which name takes precedence? Usually, the parents enjoy recounting that story as it takes them away, for the moment at least, from the medical circumstances which have brought them to the present time. Sometimes though, I sense there is still tension over the baby's name and I quickly tap dance onto another subject.

When the baby's name is not family, it often comes from a popular TV, movie, or entertainment celebrity. Since I don't keep up, my follow-up inquires allow parents to more fully explain.

I have also learned how often, in the rush and confusion of birth, a name may be mis-entered or mis-spelled on the birth certificate. An 'o' can become an 'e' or an 'a', or vice-versa. Or sometimes parents simply do the best they can with the spelling of a name they are not familiar with. By the time family realizes what has happened, the birth certificate is official and is too much bother to change.

I feel these 'name' conversations take parents, at least for a moment, away from the stress they are facing. And if I can remember it allows me to inquire how the baby is on a first name basis the next time I pass through. I hope it shows the parents that to me the baby is a real person and not just a patient.

Sometimes a name can cause a minor crisis. One story occurred when, sadly, the mom of an NICU baby, Nevaeh, decided early in her pregnancy she would not take the baby home. Mom, the only legal guardian as the dad was unknown, had told her family she would be happy if Grandma took the baby. But then the baby came early and Mom disappeared before the necessary papers could be signed. As the NICU staff and I understood things, Nevaeh was destined for foster care. This cast a deep pall over the unit. This sad situation continued for several weeks.

Then, a breakthrough!

We learned that Mom had briefly re-emerged and had signed the necessary papers. Yes! This baby who was getting close to going home did have a home to go to. Everyone was thrilled. Excited plans were made to introduce the baby to Grandma.

Then there was a setback. Grandma announced her pet dog was named Nevaeh and she would not have two Nevaeh's in her house. Guess whose name Grandma wanted changed? Gloom again!

But not for long. Suddenly, the baby had a new name—Faith. Problem solved. Smiles all around.

I missed Grandma's first meeting with the baby and then the going-home day celebration, but I was told in great detail how happy everyone was.

Just another NICU day!

Oh yes, the question at the beginning of this segment. Nevaeh, a new name to me, is Heaven spelled backwards. It is a very popular NICU name these days.

CHAPTER 13

Long Haul Baby Vance

In mid-October 2020, on my first day back in the hospital after the pandemic furlough, I finally, after wandering around the new hospital totally lost for a few minutes got two steps into the NICU when Physical Therapist Jane, without bothering to say "Welcome Back!" escorted me into a room. She pointed to the baby. "This is Vance. Make this your first stop whenever you come in. He will be here for a while."

She pointed to where the gowns and gloves were stored and began to get Baby Vance ready to be held. After she and a nurse placed him into my arms and readjusted all the lines of the various machines to which Vance was connected, said, "By the way, we missed you!"

Some welcome back! I found myself sitting and thinking. My first conversation with Vance went something like this.

"You know, Vance, it simply can't be a coincidence that an eighty-one-year old guy and an eight-day old baby are sitting here and hanging onto each other for dear life. Let's you and I figure out what's going on here."

Vance wasn't impressed with my spiritual insight. He yawned and fell asleep.

I soon learned that Vance was, indeed, a very fragile human. He was a twenty-five-week baby. This and his various other medical issues, had apparently been more than Mom could handle. The Pediatric Palliative

Care Program (PPCP) team realized there was little Mom, who lived mid-State, could do at this stage. They kept up with her, but didn't attempt to force her back into Vance's life. I suspected Pediatric Palliative Care Nurse Hallie had a 'Grand Plan', but I had no clue what it might be. I mention my take on this grim scenario as it does have something to do with how Vance's story is playing out as I write this.

Several months passed. Vance's condition ebbed and flowed. There were times he could not be held and I could only hold his hand when I was with him or just stand in the doorway and tell him to 'hang in there'. There were other times he could be held, but it would take three nurses to transfer Vance and all the things he was hooked-up to the three feet between his crib and where I was sitting. It was a very big deal, but the nurses were convinced that my holding him was even more of a big deal.

For most of these first months, Vance was with us in body, but not much else. Every time I went into the NICU, I would first take a deep breath and steady myself for whatever news might be awaiting on Baby Vance.

Four months later, I could see that Vance was joining us in this world. He would look around and even make brief eye-contact. Even I, the ultimate amateur, could see he was hooked-up to fewer machines. It now took only two nurses, sometimes one, to get him from his crib into my arms.

Then there were discussions that Vance might soon be transferred to the PICU. He soon was, and I followed him. I was amazed that several of the PICU nurses remembered me from the old hospital. They all seemed to know why I was in the PICU and that I would be coming in on Tuesdays and Fridays to be with Baby Vance. Not exactly old home week but nice to be remembered. Slowly, very slowly, Vance's progress continued.

Then there was the good news that Vance might soon be going home. I would overhear discussions, but not details, about consultations with the hospital in Vance's mid-state hometown concerning his required follow-up treatments. One day a nurse I didn't know but quickly learned was a new member of the Pediatric Palliative Care Team came in while Vance and I were 'hanging-out.'

I introduced myself. "Oh my God! You're George," she said. "I listened in on a long phone conversation between Nurse Hallie and Vance's Mom yesterday. Hallie spent the whole time taking about you and Vance."

I nodded. Nice to be talked about in any context other than, 'How do we get rid of this loser?' The nurse finished whatever she was doing and moved on.

Five minutes later, who comes steaming into the room but Nurse Hallie. "I didn't know you were here today. Can I take a picture? Vance's Mom wants to see his best friend." She snapped the picture and rushed out.

The story pace picked up. The next week I learned that Mom, Dad, and Vance's six-year old sister would be arriving soon. I could sense Nurse Hallie's plan was falling into place. Three days later when I walked into the hospital lobby, a family was at the reception desk. I could see they recognized me and I realized they had to be Vance's parents. Even Nurse Hallie couldn't have planned that! After some initial confusion, parents and PPCP team were together and Vance's going home orientation/training had begun.

Every time since, my first stop in the hospital has been in Vance's room to say hello and get a full progress report. Vance and family have totally bonded. Mom and Dad seem more comfortable and confident each time I stop by.

Then Vance caught a bad cold and was put on very strict contact precautions. The closest I could come to him was to stand in the doorway.

And now, as I do final edits on this book, Vance gone has home. But, home is now Charleston as Mom, Dad, and big sister have relocated so Vance can be closer to the hospital for follow-up visits.

Baby Vance's story continues to unfold!

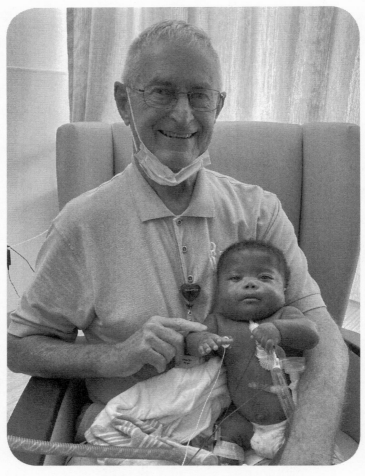

George and Baby Vance: Best Friends Forever!

How Vance's story will unfold is anybody's guess at this point in time.

CHAPTER 14

Pediatric Palliative Care (PPC)

I first became aware of the Pediatric Palliative Care Program (PPCP) through a December 2017 article in our local newspaper, The Charleston Post and Courier: 'How a Charleston Pediatrician Helps Children at the End of their Lives'. This article is far too long to copy herein but can be found on various websites.

Before this, I had been vaguely aware that there were a team of doctors, nurses, and medical and non-medical specialists who worked with the sickest, most fragile children and their families. But since these babies, by definition, could not be held, I had not followed up. The Post and Courier article changed all that. And by the way, the article and its photos did refer to doctors, nurses, and others by name, so you can for the one time in this book actually put real names to real people.

This is what I have learned since that time.

I assume the term Palliative Care rings a bell, but mostly for adults. In my review of available documentation, my amateur definition is that Palliative Care kicks-in when a patient has a condition for which there are no medical procedures, treatments, or medicines that might lead to a cure of an on-going or terminal condition. The basic goal of adult

Palliative Care is to make sure the patient is as comfortable as possible. Adult Palliative Care for adults, which most of us know as Hospice, has been around for a long time.

Pediatric Palliative Care (PPC) is a much newer medical specialty which does have a broader focus. Whereas adult Palliative Care is for adults, many of whom are in an end-of-life situation, PPC is designed for babies and children who hopefully have a long life before them. The objective of Palliative Care for both adults and children is to keep the patient stable and comfortable. But with babies and children, there is always the hope that a new medical procedure or treatment which will allow the child a chance to live a full and happy life is just around the corner. It does happen!

Children's Hospital volunteers know the benefits we personally give and receive from holding and providing comfort care to babies, children, and their families who are stuck in the hospital. We sense in addition to being ill, even the tiniest of babies are terrified. Volunteers can see our being with them for even a short period of time, reading or telling a story, singing a silly song, playing a video game, or just hanging out to watch a movie or video with older kids brings a moment of comfort and peace to those children. And we learn that parents deeply appreciate knowing someone is with their child who is stuck in the hospital. To be totally selfish, it makes us feel good to be doing something good. And it is nice that on the hospital website, the Pediatric Palliative Program page recognizes and includes volunteers as a part of their 'collaborative team'.

And yes, there are studies underway to determine the medical cost benefits to PPC. While all we have at this moment are indications, those preliminary findings are promising.

In 2014, an article in the journal, Biological Psychiatry, suggested that NICU infants who are cuddled from birth formed healthier sleep habits and showed increased attention.

Studies on the medical and monetary value of PPC are underway. Initial indications appear to show:

- PPC babies and children spend less time in the hospital than babies and children with the same condition who are not in a PPC program.
- PPC babies or children who have gone home make fewer return trips to the hospital Emergency Room than do children or babies who were not in PPC. One reason for this could be the family is included as an integral part of the child's PPC medical care team.
- Another aspect of PPC is a medical staff member of the PPC team will often do a home-visit for scheduled follow-up check-ups instead of having the baby or child come back to the hospital, a visit which may involve a couple of days in the hospital.

"What a minute!" you say. "Wouldn't that be very expensive having one person traveling maybe a full day for one visit." Apparently not when compared to having a child come into the hospital maze of expenses.

The point here is every day a baby or child who can be treated at home is at home and is not in the Emergency Room, or is not in the hospital for a follow-up, represents a huge cost saving to someone—a private insurance company, Medicaid, state or federal funding, or it simply means budget resources can be devoted to other medical demands.

Bereavement Track

Sadly though, as the cited Post and Courier article showed, not all Pediatric Palliative Care patients make it. When this sad projected outcome is medically apparent, a PPC bereavement track program comes into play. I am not directly involved in bereavement track activities as they are far above my level of competency and involvement. But I do understand they are deeply appreciated.

Grief and end of life counseling is offered to both children and parents. I have learned that children often take the sad news better than parents.

Bereavement track parents are offered help with the mountain of necessary paperwork. In some cases, the PPC team will arrange a funeral and will offer 'follow-up' services to the family.

This is one of the programs to which net proceeds from this book will be donated. Since PPC is a new evolving program, my understanding is that a number of the services provided by the PPC team are funded out-of-pocket. One example is that the PPC staff will often buy a gas card so out-of-area family members can come to the hospital for a visit. It is my goal through sales of this book to help fund these expenses.

Now, the rest of the story to the referenced Post and Courier article. It involves the grandfather who is only briefly mentioned in that piece. As it turned out, he was so impressed by the work of the PPCP staff, he became an NICU volunteer and is now one of my best friends as well.

But as I learned as I got to know him, his journey was difficult indeed. For this story, I will call him Brian.

Brian's story was that after his granddaughter, the baby in the Post and Courier story, passed away he had a terrible time with grief management. Mom, Dad, and Grandmother grieved but finally made it through the stages of grief—denial, anger, bargaining, depression, and acceptance. In fact, a couple of years after the baby passed, a new healthy and happy baby was born into the family.

Brian told me he seemed to be forever trapped in both the anger and depression stages of the grief process. Neither time, counseling, nor therapy seemed to help. He felt he was truly at the end of the line.

As a last gasp effort, he decided to fly to Spain and walk the Camino de Santiago, a network of pilgrim's trails which lead to the Cathedral of Santiago de Compostela in northwest Spain. This has been long recognized as a truly spiritual journey. Brian says he took it as a last gasp long-shot with no real expectations.

So, off he went. Brian, a successful business person, had planned well. He realized at his age that this would not be a power hike. Each day's walk would be relatively short with reserved accommodations awaiting.

The first day was a struggle. *Why am I doing this? What a fool I am. What a total waste of time,* thoughts internally raged. The first night on the trail was a struggle as well. Brian told me he tossed and turned all night thinking how crazy the whole venture was.

Still, the next morning there was really no option but to press on. So, he did. Just after mid-day, Brian came upon a young man on the trail who was re-arranging his backpack. They chatted for a moment, and the young man asked if they could walk together.

"Sure, why not."

So, they walked together for an hour or so, talking about this and that but mostly nothing. Near day's end, the young man said he had to catch up with his companions, thanked Brian for the conversation, and moved on. Even today, Brian says he cannot identify the stranger's accent.

He remembers that second night as passing a little better. He enjoyed his meal and got a decent night's sleep. Nothing really special, but different enough from the first night to make note of.

The next morning when Brian walked out of his lodging, the young man was waiting for him. And once again they walked together. Once again, they talked about this and that. And once again, in mid-afternoon, the young man pushed ahead.

Brian remembers that third night as something very special. He walked around the village where he was staying and recalls he was actually taking note of things he was seeing and experiencing. He found a restaurant and totally enjoyed a typical Spanish dinner. He went into a café where a guitarist was playing and thoroughly enjoyed the experience. He had the best night's sleep in a long, long time. He realized something special had happened.

The next morning when Brian went outside, no young man. Brian says it was at that moment he realized he had not been walking the Camino with a person. He had been in the company of an angel. His grief was behind and he was now ready to push ahead with whatever life had in store.

He completed the walk. He says he didn't expect to see the young man again, and he didn't. "I assumed he was helping someone else," Brian dryly commented.

When Brian told me this story, it gave me the shivers. Even now as I write this, it still does.

When Brian got home, he came to the Children's Hospital and signed up to volunteer. As it out turned out, I was his guide/trainer on his first shift. We quickly became fast friends; two old-timers sharing stories and facing life one half-day at a time.

Shortly after Brian began his volunteer journey, he did two things. When he had been at the hospital with his son and daughter-in-law during the baby's odyssey, he had realized there were no water dispensers in the Intensive Care family waiting rooms. If you wanted a drink of water, your options were to either go into the restroom and cup your hands under a faucet, or you could trek down eight floors to the cafeteria and pay $2 for a bottle of water. Brian remedied this situation by buying water dispensers for all Intensive Care waiting rooms.

The second thing he did was pay for the installation of charging stations in the Intensive Care family waiting rooms so parents could charge their cell phones and tablets. And a year later, Brian and his son sponsored a golf tournament which raised some $20,000 for the Pediatric Palliative Care Program.

This was all in addition to almost rivaling me as a baby whisperer.

I do believe the Pediatric Palliative Program staff have had the same positive impact on numerous families I know nothing about. And this is why PPCP is one of the programs to which I will donate a portion of net proceeds from this book.

CHAPTER 15

Long Haul Baby Ginger

Baby Ginger introduced me to the Pediatric Palliative Care Program (PPCP) team.

My understanding is that when Baby Ginger was born, the doctors did an assessment, looked at each other, shrugged their shoulders, shook their heads, and agreed this baby had so many issues, nothing could be done. So, they noted 'Keep this baby as comfortable as possible', which by definition triggered the PPCP. Baby Ginger was sent to the NICU.

In the NICU, I am told that a senior PPCP nurse reviewed the instructions and the accompanying material. Then, with the support of Mom and Dad who were both medical professionals, marched back to the doctors and said something like, "This is (insert two highly technical four-letter words, one begins with a 'B', the other with a 'S')! There is nothing here that can't be fixed. Yes, the odds are not good, but we refuse to give up on this child. We want a treatment plan, and we want it now!"

After what I am sure was a measured discussion now deeply buried in the MUSC archives, a treatment plan was produced and Baby Ginger's NICU odyssey began.

I met Baby Ginger shortly thereafter. One morning I walked into the NICU and there was Mom, a four-year old little girl (Baby Ginger's 'big sister' as it turned out), and a bevy of nurses, technicians, therapists, and transporters getting Baby Ginger prepared for what was her first procedure. The tension and stress were so thick, even I, Mr. Ultimate Oblivious, could feel it.

When the transporters began to roll Baby Ginger away, followed by Mom, the four-year broke down. I was closest to her and dropped to my knees to try and comfort the little girl. I immediately realized I didn't have a clue what to do.

So, I started talking about bacon.

George: "I love bacon. I bet you do to."

I was shocked when it seemed to get her attention. She muffled a sob and looked at me as though I were insane. I continued: "Why don't we go to the cafeteria and have a special bacon breakfast?"

Little girl, still sobbing, but not as much: "I love bacon."

George, on a roll: "How many pieces can you eat at one time?"

Little girl, wondering how far she could play this sucker: "Lots!"

At that moment, I was rescued by Mom, who had come back into the unit and had overheard the last couple of exchanges of our conversation.

Mom took the little girl's hand: "Let's go get some breakfast." She turned to me. "Can you join us?"

I begged off.

Just another day as a Baby Whisperer.

An hour or so later, Mom tracked me down, introduced herself, and thanked me profusely for saving the day. "The procedure went well," she remarked and proceeded to fill me in on Baby Ginger's situation. The only thing I really understood was there was a lot going-on.

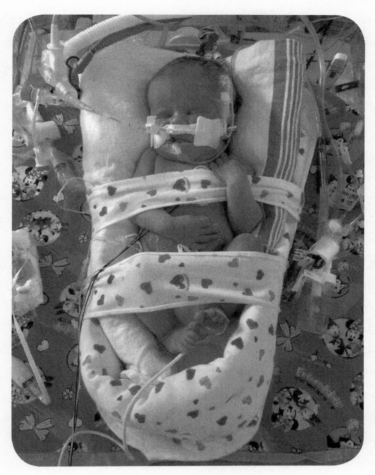

Baby Ginger: Hello world! Not what I expected.

Over time I learned that Mom and Dad, both medical professionals, were fully aware of Baby Ginger's long road ahead. They were concerned about how they could be in two places at the same time; with Baby Ginger in Charleston and with their other children and full-time medical careers in mid-state South Carolina.

All I could do was listen and promise that Baby Ginger would be my first stop every time I came into the hospital. And for almost the next full year, Baby Ginger was.

After a few weeks, a routine emerged. Mom and Dad would come to Charleston on the weekends. Granddad showed up every Tuesday morning and stayed until mid-afternoon Thursday. Granddad (R.I.P.) and I became fast friends. We took turns holding Baby Ginger while we discussed and resolved world, life, and college sports issues.

I would then be Baby Ginger's best friend forever every Friday morning.

Over the next year, procedure after procedure unfolded. I followed Ginger into the Pediatric Cardiac Intensive Unit, where frustratingly, her procedure was postponed twice—once when Mom agreed that another baby's procedure was more critical. But finally, that procedure was done, and Baby Ginger returned to the NICU.

A minor crisis was resolved when Physical Therapist Jane demanded that Baby Ginger's crib be moved to a better location, a spot with a view of outside. Baby Ginger accumulated more best friends forever in that one year than most of us will have in a lifetime.

Finally, all that remained was the one final very critical procedure. Hearts were in throats; silent prayers were said. Guess what? Baby Ginger sailed through that procedure without a glitch, at least as far as I could tell and if silly smiles all around are any measure of success.

Baby Ginger was on track to go home.

Finally, the big day arrived. Mom rented a huge van to accommodate a year's worth of accumulated stuff. Granddad and I were assigned to load the van while Mom signed the mountain of paperwork and accepted the well wishes of what seemed to be half the hospital staff. On one trip to the van, Granddad turned to me and asked, "What do you think will happen now?"

"Who knows?" I said. "All we can do is be thankful for each half-day we are given."

That philosophical discussion completed, we stuffed the van even fuller. Soon, Mom, Baby Ginger, and an entourage of well-wisher arrived, and off they went into a new life.

Here is a pic of Baby Ginger on her last day in the hospital.

Yes, there were smiles and tears all around.

And two years later, here is Big Girl Ginger.

Why volunteers hold babies.

CHAPTER 16

The Oncology Unit

Before I was assigned to the NICU, I did a stint in the Oncology Unit.
One thing I quickly noticed was that people passing by outside that unit
would literally move to the other side of the hall when they saw the Pediatric
Oncology sign. Nobody wanted anything to do with oncology. At the old
hospital, that sign was finally removed and replaced by...nothing. I suppose
those who were in charge thought people who were going to that unit knew
where they were going or would find it sooner or later. Others just passing
by simply didn't need to face the oncology word and its implications.

In the new hospital, the Oncology Unit, now renamed the Cancer
Unit, is on the top floor—out of sight and out of the way to all but those
who must be there. Nobody gets off the elevator on that floor unless it is
where they want to go or must go.

Once I started volunteering, I realized the Oncology Unit experienced
the highest staff turnover of any unit in the hospital. I soon understood
why. While the Oncology Unit is where one does see miracles, it is also
sometimes a seemingly endless succession of heart-breaking events. Thank
goodness there are doctors, nurses and other medical staff who were born to
work in that unit, just as I now believe I was born to be a Baby Whisperer.
I am in awe of them! But for a lot of staff, including guess who, there is a
moment one decides they must move on.

Still, it is all about the children and the babies. The very good news is that, even in the Oncology Unit, miracles occur and the kids go home. But not always.

As volunteers, we are faced with both situations.

Here are some of my Oncology Unit stories, some happy, some sad.

Oncology Story: Shasa

Baby Shasa was born with a cancer so rare, I learned only a few cases had been recorded in South Carolina, and of those before Baby Shasa, most had passed away soon after birth.

A nurse remarked to me, "I worked on that child when she was two days old. I remember saying to myself this would most likely be the only time I would be with her."

To make a sad story even more tragic, Baby Shasa's family situation was incredibly bizarre. A court order was in effect prohibiting every member of her family, including grandparents, from even coming into the hospital. There was one time when the Oncology Unit had to go onto 'lock-down" when it was feared a family member had slipped into the hospital. Baby Shasa was as alone as alone could be.

But Baby Shasa was a fighter. She lived for almost a year. The Oncology Unit was her home. Volunteers, doctors, nurses, social workers, and staff from all over the hospital became her surrogate family. I worked with my boss, Volunteer Coordinator Chris, to organize volunteers so that at least two volunteers would be with Baby Shasa for at least a couple of hours every day. This was the first glimpse of a program called Gentle Journey, which I like to think was a predecessor to the Pediatric Palliative Care Program. Note: Go to https://depthtml.musc.edu/catalyst/2010/co3-12program.html for a story on the Gentle Journey program and a picture of a much younger George.

When I was with Baby Shasa, and when she was up for it, I would open her door, pull a chair into the opening, gather her up along with all the tubes, lines, and monitor contacts she was connected to, and we would sit and watch the people go by. She loved it. I think it reached the point where no one would come close to the Oncology Unit without making a detour to stop and say hello to Baby Shasa. But as with many babies in the hospital, I never saw a smile, or even the beginnings of one, from this child.

But alas, her condition was untreatable and incurable. Shortly before she was one year old, she passed. I helped organize a Remembrance Service at the Chapel on the hospital campus. The chapel was full. The service was beautiful. Folks I had never seen before came forward and told moving stories about their time with Baby Shasa. Afterwards, we all filed into the courtyard. After a short prayer, we released balloons and watched them float into the heavens. It seemed to allow us to release our grief. It was moving. Then, it was back to the unit!

By the way, a bit further on in my chapter on nurses and in my Dedication, and probably in several other places, you will see a phrase something like, "The Children's Hospital medical staff are the most caring, compassionate, and competent group of professionals I have ever worked with." Believe it!

Baby Shasa's story is just one example.

Oncology Story: Kalia

I was with Kalia who ended up in the Pediatric Oncology Unit three different times. She would come, stay for three months or so while she received treatment, be declared cancer free or in remission, and go home. Six months to a year later, she would be back and go through the same difficult process. After her third trip through Oncology, when she must have been around seven years old, she was declared cancer free and went home. As far as I know, she never came back.

I got to know Kalia well. She loved to sit with me at the nurse's station where she would, in a sweet way, boss everyone around. She and the nurses made a game of guessing how her hair would come back, after radiation. They discussed it endlessly. Would it be brown or blonde? Would it be curly or straight? And for her hair, the third time was a charm. It was brown and curly—really curly with super tight curls. Kalia was thrilled.

Just before she went home for the last time, we were sitting in her room talking about this and that. I said, "You know, Kalia, when you get older, you should come back as a candy striper.

Kalia: "What's a candy striper?"

Me, always seeking ways to extend conversations during my three-hour shift: "Why don't you ask the nurses when they come in?"

So, for the next hour or so, every time a nurse came in, Kalia would ask, "What's a candy striper?"

And in almost every instance, the nurse would respond with a huge smile and something like, "Oh, that's how I got started. It was wonderful," followed by a story.

Finally, I said, "You see Kalia, nobody knows more than you about what it's like to be a sick kid in the hospital. If you were a candy striper, you could make a big difference for other sick kids here."

With that, she looked me in the eye, and with total conviction, and absolutely no doubt said, "When I get out of this place, I ain't never coming back!"

A few moments later, she asked, "What's so funny?"

The best I could do was to say, "Kalia, I understand completely. Your ticket has been punched." I then spent the rest of my shift trying to explain what 'Your ticket has been punched' meant.

Conversation with a Pediatric Oncology Doctor

One day, I saw a doctor in the halls of the unit who was shuffling his feet and shifting papers from one hand to the other as he waited for test results.

Me: "Can I ask you a question?"

Doctor: "Sure."

Me: "How is it that you can cure so many kids with leukemia. But when old codgers like me get it, we are usually done for?"

Doctor, looking around to be sure no one was in hearing range: "Pure blind luck!"

Me: "Huh!"

Doctor: "You've got to realize that these treatments are a chemical cocktail and there are an infinite number of possible combinations. It was pure luck we hit on one that works on kids with this type of leukemia, at least until they are around three years old. That same cocktail doesn't work when they get older."

Me: "That must be frustrating."

Doctor: "You better believe it! We were sure we would figure out a tweak so it would work on older kids." He paused before continuing. "But no luck yet." He paused again, looked around, then continued. "But we will keep on trying and someday..."

Just then the test results he had been awaiting arrived, and off he went.

Oncology Story: Little Girl Daisy

The Oncology Unit in the old hospital had rooms which were reverse pressurized and were mostly used for oncology patients who had surgery and simply couldn't be put into a situation where they might pick up an infection. In my experience, it was mostly kids who had had organ transplants or whose immune systems were damaged.

One day I was sitting in the reverse pressure room with Daisy, who was five years old. Her transplant had been a success, and she was ready to play. So, we had a tea party. We took modeling clay and made cups, saucers, cookies and small cakes. Whenever anyone came into the room, they were invited to join the tea party. Daisy was thrilled.

Then, in a moment when we were alone, an ambulance or police car, passed outside, siren on full blast. Daisy looked at me and with a serious expression said, "They're coming for you!"

"Oh no!" I replied. "I'll hide under the bed."

She gave me an even more serious expression: "My daddy tried that and it didn't work."

What would have been your response to that?

When I finished my shift and went back into the unit, I told the nurses. "We knew something was up with that family," one said.

Another 'Reverse Pressure Room' story. I was sitting with a very small little girl who was recovering from transplant surgery. She was basically 'out of it,' but there was one moment when she grabbed my finger and would not let go. When I went back to the nurse's station desk, I remarked on that incident.

"George, you have to realize these kids are giving it everything they have. Their instinct to live is incredible."

My next time back, when I inquired, all I got was a sad shake of a head. The little girl hadn't made it. Even so, her grabbing my finger and holding it for dear life has stuck with me ever since.

Oncology Story: Alma and Louise

One day I was sitting with Alma, who was eight years old. She was in treatment and looked just about as bad as bad can be. But she was in great spirits.

Me: "I'm impressed by your attitude. Good for you."

Alma: "Oh, it's because of Louise. She's my best friend here and she is two treatments ahead of me. She tells me all about how it's going to be and what I'll feel like. She tells me if she can take it, then I can to. Have you met her yet?"

Me: "Not yet, but when I do, I'll tell her you said hello."

A few minutes later, Alma was taken away for a procedure. I went looking for Louise.

The 'look' I got from my inquiry at the nurses' station told me this was not good.

Nurse: "Louise is having a very hard time," one nurse said. Then after a debate among the assembled staff, "You can stick your head in the door."

Another Nurse: "Please! See if you can get Mom to take a break. Anything to get her out of the room. She won't leave and is running everyone here crazy, including herself and Louise."

"Including us!" Another nurse exclaimed. This brought a chorus of nods.

So, off I went. I knocked on the door and slipped in. The room was dark, but I could see a form in the bed. Mom, sitting on the sofa, looked like she had been run through the wringer, many times. I sat next to her, introduced myself, and told her how Alma had asked me to drop by and say hello to her best friend Louise.

Mom said, "I think she's awake and would like that."

I got up and moved over to the bed.

It still hurts me to think how terrible that child looked. I don't think I've ever seen anyone sicker. But she was awake. I took her hand and told her what Alma had said about her being able to handle the treatments because her best friend Louise had told her she could. I told her that Alma, and I, thought she was an Angel.

Louise tried to manage a smile and she squeezed my hand. "Tell her hello," was the best she could do. She drifted off to sleep. I held her hand for a moment and then walked back to Mom and told her my Alma story.

Then I remembered the nurse's instructions. "Look," I said, "why don't you take a walk around the block? It's a beautiful day. You need a break. I'll sit here with Louise until you get back."

"No!" Mom exclaimed so fervently, I took a step back. "The doctors only come by once a day. I know if I leave the room, that will be when they come. I'll miss out on what's going on with Louise."

That made sense to me, so I tried another track. "Okay, why don't you slip into the bathroom, take a quick shower and get some fresh clothes on. I'll stay right here. If the doctors come, I'll personally block the door so they can't leave before you get out."

It took more coaxing, but finally she disappeared into the bathroom and took what must have been the quickest shower in history. I cracked the room door open so anyone walking by could see me standing by Louise's bed. Mom looked so much better when she emerged. And thankfully, no doctor appeared so I didn't have to throw my body across the door.

I briefed the nurses and headed to the Volunteer Office where I announced I had done my last shift in Oncology. "More than I can handle," I said.

It turned out I had lasted longer than most, as Oncology Unit volunteer tours are known for fast burn-out rates. "I think you'll like the NICU," the Volunteer Coordinator said.

CHAPTER 17

Into the World of Intensive Care

In poll after poll, the hospital system where I volunteer is chosen as the best place to work in the Charleston area. I have come to believe that the medical staff I work with in the Intensive Care Units exemplifies this vote. They are there because there is no other place they want to be.

I am not sure about everybody, but I do know the nurses and many of the therapists work twelve-hour shifts spread over a seven-day (not Monday-Friday) week, with night-shifts thrown in to boot. I understand there are those who prefer the night-shift, but just imagine someone used to working day-shifts being told, "We need you to do a night-shift for the next couple of weeks."

Oh yes, holidays are included. If your name comes up for the 'Team' working Christmas or Thanksgiving, well, you have to figure out how to re-schedule dinners, opening presents, and sort out family issues.

Hurricanes? What hurricanes?? The hospital never closes. A designated team comes and stays the course. Everyone has their secret sleeping place. Hurricane and holiday stories, some not appropriate for this book, abound.

The point is that any of these folks could get a Monday-Friday nine-to-five job that pays the same salary. But they don't. Why? Because they know the Children's Hospital is where they are supposed to be.

Now, a George definition of the three Pediatric Intensive Care Units, now called Critical Care Units in the hospital.

The Pediatric Intensive Care Unit (PICU) is for children up to eighteen years old. I have volunteered in the PICU a number of times, usually when I follow a baby who has moved from the NICU. And when I sometimes drop by the PICU to say hello to the nurses and staff, they will often gently, but firmly, lead me to a child who needs a volunteer, now.

As discussed elsewhere, the Neonatal Intensive Care Unit (NICU), where I spend most of my volunteer time, is for newborn babies up to twenty-eight days old. As for the annual number of NICU patients, the hospital website notes "approximately 900 admissions to our intensive care nurseries. Neonatal transports account for 40 percent of the total admissions to our NICU." Nationwide, various published studies estimate between 300,000-500,000 babies are admitted to a NICU each year. The wide range of estimates apparently stems from different studies reviewing different aspects of NICU life. Still, it is a huge annual number.

But it often happens that NICU babies stay in the NICU sometimes for several days and sometimes for several months until they are ready to go home or move to another hospital unit. This is a medical decision. When I asked, I was told, "We understand full well the formal definitions, but these babies will be where we think they should be."

The Pediatric Cardiac Intensive Care Unit (PCICU) is for babies and children with heart issues. I see on the web that up to one percent of all babies born in the US have heart issues. Moms have told me stories of their babies having heart surgery while still in the womb. Others talk about their babies being taken away immediately after birth, then returned to Mom's arms an hour later after a heart procedure. It is amazing stuff for me, a volunteer. And while I don't usually go into the PCICU, I often follow babies who start off in the NICU, then move to the PCICU for a procedure, then come back to the NICU or PICU after that procedure.

And a note I will reinforce several times herein: Medical staff never, ever discuss a baby's medical situation with me. I am told only 'what I need to know' when holding a baby; things like, "George, this baby spits-up almost anything that hits its stomach, so be ready with this wash cloth" or "George, keep a sharp eye on the oxygen level and be sure the baby's head is positioned so it can breathe easily." That being said, after a number of years and many visits to the inter-web to learn from available information, I can sometimes pick up a sense of what's going on with a baby. And there have been times when parents, desperate to have someone to tell their story to, tell me their baby's medical history from the moment of conception until the present moment. Information like this, as well as any hallway chatter I might overhear, immediately goes into the 'file and forget' basket.

But while I spend time in all three Intensive Care Units, my heart is in the NICU, where I spend most of my time when at the hospital.

In the beginning, the NICU was a new experience.

One of the first things I had to learn was, basically, who was who. Everyone who works in the unit, from doctors to lowly volunteers wears different color 'scrubs.' It supposedly helps staff and parents know who is who and what their job is. The problem is, nobody gives the parents a list and by the time they figure it all out, they and the baby are long gone. And, this is why I always identify myself as a volunteer when I first meet parents. Otherwise, I will be hit with a barrage of medical questions.

But in case you are wondering, here is a partial color code for the Hospital where I volunteer. I hope you never have a first-hand need to know them:

Nurses	Royal Blue
Physical Therapists	Steel Gray
Occupational Therapists	Red
Respiratory Therapists	Caribbean Blue
Speech Pathologists	Mist Gray
Lactation Specialists	Lavender*
Nursing Students	White
Volunteers	Turquoise

---

* George's choice for best color selection

When I first started working in the NICU, whenever I came in, everything seemed the same, except, except... It felt like the movie *Groundhog Day* when Bill Murray would wake-up at the same time every day, and began to repeat the previous day, except each new day always unfolded differently.

It quickly struck me that in the NICU, each time I came in there would be an entirely new cast of staff characters rushing about. Finally (I can be a slow learner), I realized that NICU nurses, and all MUSC Hospital nurses, were faced with filling fourteen twelve hour shifts a week. Sure, most nurses work either day or night shifts, but still the question was 'How do you get to an average 40-hour week?'

The obvious answer is you work three 12-hour shifts one week and four 12-hour shifts the second week, or some combination thereof. Over time, it averages out to a 40-hour week. And when Saturdays, Sundays and holidays are factored in, it is no wonder a volunteer coming in once a week always seems to be wandering into a Groundhog Day situation.

However, other than that, I felt totally at ease, totally welcomed, and totally at home from the first day I walked into the NICU.

The NICU in the old Children's Hospital—we moved to the new Children's Hospital in February 2019, just before the Pandemic resulted in volunteers being furloughed for the longest seven months I can remember— was actually located in two separate buildings with two separate units in each building. Most of these units were essentially open bays. Two units had one room where as many as four babies could be placed. The nurses called those rooms Siberia because they felt cut off from the rest of the unit. Whenever they needed to take a bathroom break or even slip out to pick up supplies, they had to either flag someone down who was passing by or call someone on their cell phone to come in and relieve them.

On one of my first NICU tours, I noticed a nurse hovering over a baby in Siberia. I recognized her as someone I knew and walked in to say hello. We chatted as I walked around, not paying much attention. Then I looked closer. The following conversation took place:

George: "Jace, that baby... That baby is..." I couldn't finish.

Jace, who was brushing the baby's hair and carefully arranging a beautiful pink dress: "George, this baby is in a far better place."

George: "But, but... Why are you...?" I nodded to Jace's carefully working with the baby.

Jace: "When the parents realized what had happened, they were so distraught, they rushed out of the room. I think they will be back and I want them to see and remember this child as the beautiful little girl she is."

With that, she made a final tuck and swept out of the room. It took me a several minutes to regain my composure. When I walked into the unit, the first thing I saw was Jace totally chewing out another nurse for some transgression. It didn't take me long to learn in the NICU, one has to compartmentalize each and every event. I also quickly learned that anyone assigned to the NICU who didn't fit in, who lost focus on the job at hand, or who simply seemed to make too many unforced errors would quietly, privately, and unofficially be find a position in another unit.

As for Jace, I soon learned that with her, there was a right way to do things and a wrong way. She did not waste time or words when she saw something she thought was not being done correctly.

I was hooked.

I quickly learned nurses and therapists were the cornerstone of the Intensive Care Units. They were responsible for the minute-by-minute care and treatment of the babies. Yes, doctors make the diagnosis, write the orders, and are the overall managers of the operation, but nurses and therapists do the heavy lifting.

One of the most frequent questions I get is, "What do nurses talk about in the NICU?" The answer is simple: shoes.

Shoes! Well, think about it. Nurses are on their feet for most of a twelve-hour shift. Comfortable, and hopefully stylish, shoes are a critical necessity. One nurse told me that during the pandemic, word spread that a certain brand of clogs were perfect for an on-your-feet existence. She said for a couple of weeks the halls were alive with the sounds of clattering clogs. Other discussion topics are children's dentists, restaurants, and vacation spots. Disney World is an always favorite.

When a nurse is not with a baby, they are most likely hovering over their computer, either charting—lots of naughty words to be heard whenever hospital administration installs a new charting system—or studying for the next level nursing degree. I have learned there are four levels of nursing degrees, a two-year entry level of Associate Degree/Registered Nurse (RN), followed by a Bachelor's Degree in Nursing (BSN), then a Master's Degree (Nurse Practitioner), and finally a Doctor's Degree in Nursing (DNP). Nurses know there is always more to learn and the more they know, the better they can care of the babies.

But as you might imagine, nurses come with different personalities, different gifts, and different stories. One such nurse, Gabby, now retired, impressed me as the moral compass of the NICU. Against all advice, Gabby would give her home phone number to troubled moms and would receive calls at all times of the night or day. When Gabby reported back on these calls, which to me always seemed to be made at 3:00 AM, there was a combination of admiration and exasperation all around.

And woe be onto any unclear or contradictive medical or administrative directive. But often, after a scorched earth approach at making something right, Gabby would show up with waffle iron, containers of waffle batter, butter and syrup, and cook waffles for the entire NICU team. My only contribution to this was to impress upon her that she should only do waffles on Tuesdays or Fridays as those are my volunteer days. I always knew when she was doing waffles. When I walked into the unit, nurses would approach me and say, "Please go to the break room for your waffle so Gabby will stop ranting about you." Hospital nurse humor, right?

Speaking of hospital nurse humor, I was recently tapped to open a ZOOM meeting for another local organization I am involved with. I thought I had made it clear: 'No problem as long as it isn't on a Tuesday or Friday morning. Those are my hospital days.' Naturally, the meeting was set for a Tuesday morning. After spirited negotiations, I committed two ZOOM minutes to open the meeting, thank the participants for attending, and then to turn the meeting over to some else.

On the morning of the meeting, I approached the unit charge nurse who was chatting with other nurses. "Where is your 'hidey-hole' where you go to make a 'super-secret' phone call that is nobody else's business?" I inquired.

"George, I am truly shocked you would even think I would know such a thing," she announced to the world while at the same time walking away and motioning for me to follow.

We proceeded down the hall to a storage room filled with equipment, furniture, and boxes. I followed as she navigated to a spot deep into the room where a chair and small table were well hidden from sight. "Here," she said and walked away.

I sat and started to pull ZOOM up on my phone, but I saw she had returned. "George," she said while wagging a finger into my face, "don't you dare have a heart attack and die in here. It will be six months before anyone finds you." With that she was gone. I made my call, sixty-six seconds, and was soon holding a baby.

Later that morning, I was telling that story to Nurse Pat, who laughed and remarked. "That's exactly what happened during the last hurricane lock-down. A maintenance worker went missing. We turned the hospital upside down looking for him. And guess what? He had slipped into an equipment storage room to sleep and had a heart attack. He's back now, but…"

Speaking of Nurse Pat, she has a truly special gift. She can find a vein in even the tiniest baby so a line can be put into use. Being able to find a vein is an incredible gift. I have seen nurses break into tears of frustration and have learned many new words when jab after jab after jab was fruitless.

My role in a situation like this is to either get out of the way, or when asked, help hold the baby as still as possible while the nurse searches for a vein. One time, in a very difficult situation where I was observing a nurse unsuccessfully look for a vein and on the verge of both naughty words and tears, I said, "I'm going to find Nurse Pat." Luckily, she was just down the hall.

"Can you please come help?" I asked.

"Lead on," she replied, and back we went. My job was the same; help keep the baby still. As Nurse Pat worked, I learned that this baby, a new-born who had initially seemed to be in great shape, had been transferred to the NICU in the middle of the night when things began to go wrong. The baby's mom had finally dropped off to sleep, and it was decided not to wake her as there was nothing she could do but fret and worry.

But now Mom was awake and just outside the unit demanding to be allowed to be with her baby. "Keep her outside, and I'll handle her when I finish this," Nurse Pat said and continued to seek a vein. But this time, even she was having problems. Everyone was really tense, and we could hear Mom outside demanding to be let in. Nurse Pat simply kept trying.

Then, she glanced at me. "George, you're white as a sheet," she said. "Don't you dare pass out on me. Either shut your eyes or look at the ceiling."

Finally, probably not nearly as long as it seemed, success! Nurse Pat accepted her due acclaim with appropriate modestly and went out to calm Mom down so she could come in and hold her baby. To this day, I'm not sure who needed holding more, the baby or me. I was a wreck as I still get weak-kneed whenever someone approaches me with a needle.

And speaking of holding—another nurse story:

On one of my first days back in the hospital after our seven-month pandemic furlough, I was patiently waiting for a nurse to prepare a baby she wanted me to hold—diaper changed, blanket adjusted, all lines perfectly positioned, monitoring tabs just so.

"So, how are things with you?" I asked as she worked away.

"Actually, not that good," she responded. "Two days ago, my husband had to go into ten-day isolation when a work colleague tested positive for the Covid." She paused, "He did not take it well when I banished him to the guest bedroom."

She continued to work with the baby. "Then, last night when I was putting our eight-year old to bed, I happened to look at his cell phone. I was stunned at the filth on it. There was nothing we could do last night, but that's what I am going home to this evening."

She turned and looked at me. "To hell with the baby. I need someone to hold me." Simultaneously, we said, "Now, that's really a bad idea." A week or so later when I ran into her, I asked, "So, how are things going?"

She laughed and said, "Better!"

Every nurse has their own story, but I can fully agree with survey after survey which finds nurses are one of the most respected professions.

CHAPTER 18

The NICU: It's a Woman's World

Against the advice of some, 'You do realize somebody will be upset', I am adding this chapter.

What has struck me as I sit, hold babies, and observe the Intensive Care world unfolding around me, and as I mention several times herein, reflect on how incredibly fortunate I am to be with associated with the most caring, the most compassionate, and by far the most competent group of professionals I have ever known, is how many are women. In fact, my unofficial reckoning is that well over 95% of the Intensive Care Unit staffs are female.

Of the fifteen neonatal doctors listed on the hospital website, twelve are women. One of these doctors tells me she has worked at this NICU for over forty years, has taken care of more than 35,000 babies, and has no plans to retire. Another, who has only been at the NICU for ten years but has moved up from this being a first job to now managing the NICU, tells me she can't wait for this book. "When people ask me what I do, I'm not sure what to say. I know they don't want the technical medical stuff. I'll just hand them a copy of your book and tell them to read it."

An informal review of information on the hospital website indicates that approximately two thirds of the Pediatric Resident are woman. Note:

Residents are doctors who have just graduated from medical school. The Pediatric Residency is a three-year program where doctors, still under supervision, put into practice everything they have learned in four years of pre-med and four years of medical school. After the three year of Residency, they will either go into basic pediatric medical practice or continue their pediatric training in various special fields. Another decision they must make at some point in their training is whether to go into clinical medicine where they work directly with patients, or go into research. One doctor tells me he needed an additional three years of pediatric training after his three-year residency before he was qualified to work as a Neonatal Physician. And, recently as I was holding a baby, a doctor came in and introduced herself as almost finished up on a three-year fellowship. I inquired, "What happens next? Do you have a job, or are you looking?"

"Actually, neither," she replied. "I am so totally exhausted all I want to do is go be alone somewhere and pull myself back together." She paused, "There are plenty of good jobs out there, and I may decide on going into research, but for now..." she trailed off, and walked out of the room. Two minutes later, she was back. "Please, please don't tell a soul what I just said."

"I'm sorry. Have we met?" I asked.

I think she smiled, but can't be sure as she was masked-up.

Still, that is an amazing amount of study and training just to qualify for a first job.

Informal discussions with NICU and PICU nurses led to a consensus that at least ninety-five percent of nurses in those two units are women. My observations lead me to conclude that 100% of NICU physical therapists, occupational therapists, and lactation therapists at this time, in this hospital where I volunteer are women. The one exception to this is, maybe, half the respiratory therapists are men.

Most all nursing students I see passing though the units on various training or orientation assignments are women. When I chat with the few male nursing students, I learn many had been military medics who are now studying nursing with plans to 're-up' as an officer once they get their nursing degree. This is of particular interest to me as in 1962, I spent twelve weeks at Fort Sam Houston in San Antonio, Texas, for basic combat-medic training. I have learned that Fort Sam Houston is still the primary military medic training facility, but that sadly, most of the beer joints and Mexican restaurants I frequented all those years ago are long gone.

And volunteers? Of the some one-hundred volunteers assigned to the intensive care units, I can count the number of guys on one hand with fingers left over. Just this morning the nurse who was preparing a baby for me to hold ask, "Do remember training my sister Katie five years ago? She was in Pharmacy School then."

I drew a blank. "What was her name?"

"Katie."

"To be honest. I'm not sure." I changed the subject. "Where is she now?"

"She has a great job in Kentucky." The nurse paused. "She said you and Rob were the only two male volunteers in the NICU, so it had to be one of you."

"Sure," I said with fingers crossed behind my back. "I remember her. Please pass her my best and congratulations."

So, you ask, what's your point? My point is I am happy, pleased, and proud to be a small part—the bottom rung of a bureaucratic ladder actually—of this organization which is, in fact, a woman's world and one where I feel totally welcomed, totally at home and a totally accepted member of the team.

Now, back to the babies.

CHAPTER 19

A NICU Shift Unfolds

As mentioned in other chapters, I basically arrive at the hospital, sign in at the volunteer office for my three-hour shift, make my way to the NICU (sometimes with 'stop-offs' in other units to say 'hello') and find a baby to hold.

Sometimes, finding a baby isn't as easy as it might seem. I have learned that asking nurses if they know where such babies are isn't always successful. This is mainly because NICU nurses are assigned to, at most, two babies on any given shift. If it turns out that one of their babies does need to be held, well, there you are. But since each nurse is totally focused on their assigned babies, they usually don't have information on the other babies in the unit.

One interesting thing about the new hospital is that there is a large TV screen at the charge nurse station where all babies, along with assigned nurses, are listed. On any given day, there are between 70-90 babies in the NICU. The NICU is officially 'full' when there are 82 babies 'in-residence.' I have asked, but there seems to be, with two exceptions, neither rhyme nor reason why that number will jump around. Nurses are convinced you can expect an immediate patient increase after a major winter or summer weather event with low barometric pressure, or nine months after a major power outage. Today, when I checked, there were 84

NICU patients. When I made a comment, the charge nurse said, "This is the new normal."

I have noted, however, that if the number of patients drops below 70, some nurses get nervous as someone may be told don't bother to come in. If the number surpasses 90, then a scramble ensues to find space for the overflow. NICU staff can be very inventive when this happens. Rooms designed for one baby can be re-arranged to take two, or rooms set-aside for storage can be emptied, cleaned, and used.

But back to George finding a baby. Over time, I have learned to track down either a physical therapist (steel gray shirt) or an occupational therapist (red shirt). They know the unit, and they know the babies as they spend, say, thirty-minute therapy sessions with a large number of babies during their shift. They also know the babies who can be held or need to be held. I hope I am not jinxing myself, but I cannot remember when I didn't find a baby to hold. On the other hand, wouldn't it be nice if George showed up and there were no babies in the NICU at all, or if every baby there did have a parent or guardian?

So, George shows up and finds a baby; then what?

First, the infection control procedure. Always, always, there is a two-minute soap and hot water finger-tips to elbows scrub. This is followed by finding and putting a fresh pillow-case on the pillow I use to support the baby's head. I then find and don a clean gown and, if instructed by the nurse, surgical gloves. Since the pandemic, everyone wears a mask.

The nurse then hands me the baby. Although I know some volunteers are comfortable handling a baby from crib to arms and then back to the crib, I always ask the nurse to both hand me the baby and then take the baby away.

Early in my volunteering career, I would do this myself if the nurse gave the okay. But one day when a baby and I were having a wonderful time together, I suddenly realized my pants were soaking wet. Something had come unplugged, and fluids supposedly going into the baby had found another home.

This turned out to be a very big deal. I learned that fluids going into and coming out of a baby are measured and weighed to the last milliliter. Nurses even weigh a changed baby's diapers. I could see this nurse was very upset even though she tried to put her best face possible on the situation. "It happens," she said, but she couldn't quite reach a smile.

Since that time, unless the nurse insists (which they sometimes do when they can't break away to hand me the baby), I will ask the nurse to hand and take away the baby. I figure if something comes loose or un-plugged, we can share the blame. Thank goodness, it hasn't happened since that one time.

So, once situated, George and the baby are ready to become best friends forever. I sing to the baby. I talk to the baby. I comfort the baby.

Most importantly, since I am a story-teller, I tell stories. In my stories, the baby is always the star, and the baby's name is mentioned in every paragraph.

For little boys, the stories are about stomping in mud puddles, throwing rocks and sticks, climbing trees, hunting, fishing, or riding in the back of a red Dodge Ram pick-up truck. One little boy wouldn't listen to the story unless it was a red Dodge Ram pick-up, so since then that is what they are. Basically, I build my story around everything I loved to do when I was a little boy.

When I am holding a baby girl, I tell stories about organizing and hosting a tea party or my two-hour special story about the little girl (of course, the little girl's name is the same as the baby) waking-up from her nap and while enjoying a cookie and glass of milk, wonders if a princess lives on their street. The little girl wants to know, and know now. Mom says, "Let's take a walk and ask our neighbors."

Their walks begins. The little girl meets and asks all the neighbors. Each neighbor has their own story about the princess. During my story, every time a nurse, therapists, doctor, or cleaning lady comes into the room, they immediately become part of the story. Finally, finally (when my shift is just about over) the little girl realizes she is the princess. Happy ending!

Now, in fact, the baby I am holding has usually fallen fast asleep within ten minutes of our coming together. But such a minor inconvenience will never deter a true story teller. The baby who has come to me with fists clinched, terrified eyes, and shoulder muscles tighter than ropes is now limper than a wet dishrag. I believe that baby knows instinctively that it is safe, it is sound, that while with me nobody will stick it or prick it, and nobody will stick a tube up their nose. That baby is long-gone. Does this stop me from telling my story? Of course not. I am a story teller. It is what I do.

While I am telling my story, I am sitting and observing the NICU world pass by and unfold before me. I have realized I can learn so much by simply sitting, observing, and asking anyone who comes into the room, "What's new?"

CHAPTER 20

The Darker Side

Elsewhere I have mentioned that I intersperse heart-warming and heart-wrenching stories because life in the NICU does include both.

One such heart-wrenching issue is Foster Care.

One day in the old hospital soon after I had just started working in the NICU, the unit door opened and a heavily armed uniformed policeman walked in. He looked around and walked out. Five minutes later, the doors swung open again and two policemen, both armed, escorted a young woman into the unit.

The woman was in chains. She was handcuffed, and the handcuffs were locked onto a wide leather belt. Her feet were shackled as well. At best, she could only shuffle. This NICU unit had a big open bay with one small room normally used either for babies ready to go home, for babies who the nurses wanted to shelter from any infection that might be floating around the unit, or for overflow space when there simply wasn't enough space for another baby in the bay. The police escorted the woman into this room.

Five minutes later, they were gone.

"What was that all about?" I asked the unit Charge Nurse who happened to be standing next to me observing this very unusual event.

She shrugged as though it were just another NICU day. "She's an inmate in the State Woman's prison. Her husband is also in prison. They are both there for a long time. This is probably the only time she will see the baby." She turned to leave but stopped and continued. "If there is anything good about all this, that woman's sister, the baby's aunt, has agreed to take the baby."

The next time I came in, the feel in the unit was different. It turned out the woman-in-chains had written a terrible letter to her sister threatening her with all sorts of mayhem. The sister, probably wisely, backed away from her offer to take the baby.

The nurses were despondent. "This means the baby will have to go into foster care!" one wailed. This was my introduction to foster care.

It didn't take long for me to realize that the most upsetting event that can happen in the NICU isn't when a baby passes away. Nurses and medical staff have been trained for such an occurrence. It is difficult. It is hard. But it does happen. All they can do is say a small prayer as there will be a new baby to take care of soon enough.

In fact, some nine hundred babies are admitted each year to the children's hospital neonatal and cardiac intensive care units. While statistics for the MUSC hospital are not available, if one applies the national average of deaths per 100,000 babies in intensive care units, less than ½ of one percent, this would indicate very few babies in this NICU don't make it.

As for me, whenever I come into the NICU and see a baby I have been holding is not there, I don't ask. Sometimes, a nurse will mention that the baby either went home or was transferred to another unit. I don't recall ever being told, "George, that child didn't make it."

What does cast a pallor of gloom over the NICU is when it becomes apparent that a baby who is ready to go home doesn't have a home to go home to. Foster care is the only option. On one occasion, I actually felt the nurses were so upset they weren't focusing on their assigned babies. So, I, the rank amateur, spoke to the charge nurse. She immediately sorted that issue out without, thank goodness, mentioning me.

One somewhat positive, foster care story: When I volunteered in Oncology, I spent time with a darling little boy, maybe three years old. I learned he had been born with a cancerous brain tumor that was pressing against his optic nerve. So, doctors had a double challenge: remove the tumor and do so without damaging the optic nerve.

One day, we were sitting together in the Nurses Station—little folks do love to hang-out there—when the little boy's mom called. The nurse brought the phone over and I could hear one side of a sweet conversation. "I love you Mommy. When are you coming to see me? I want to go home."

After a moment, the nurse took the phone and resumed her conversation with mom. Then, the nurse hung up the phone, and I could see she was crying. I got the little boy, Chris, back into his room and settled, then went to see what had happened. It turned out mom had announced she simply could not take her son back and was giving him up to foster care. Talk about an ice-cold wet blanket!

But there was a somewhat happy ending to this story, at least as I was following it. There are foster parents who are trained to accept medically fragile children. And in this instance, Chris hit the jackpot. Twice, I saw Chris and his foster parents on his check-up visits to the Oncology Unit. If there is a definition for angels on earth, those two foster parents would be the prime examples. Chris went on and on about all the wonderful things they did together. He could not have been happier.

But I have learned that foster care is near the bottom rung on the child care ladder. The South Carolina foster care system, managed by the SC Department of Social Service (DSS), is under staffed, over loaded and underfunded. There are more children in the system than families prepared to take them. Many of these children end up in group foster homes, an even worse situation.

I have also learned that the DSS is composed of folks with huge hearts working in a virtually impossible situation. By the time they get to work each morning, their carefully planned schedule has been overtaken by events. They begin the day running late. Then, they learn a court order has been signed and everything must be dropped. Long scheduled meetings with families have to be cancelled and rescheduled. Everybody is upset and angry, which is exactly what one doesn't want when working with children who realize they have been rejected or abandoned or removed from their families by court order. I have great sympathy for those folks.

The more positive news is I learned of, visited, and spoke with that a number of local non-profit organizations devoted to making life easier for these children. They offer food pantries, clothes, toys, games, and school supplies the children can select. Some local churches offer baby-sitting so foster parents can take a break.

I also learned about an organization HALOS (www.charlestonhalos.org) which works to place foster care designated kids with kinship relationships—grandparents, aunts, uncles, even older siblings. In fact, in South Carolina today, some 69,000 kids are living in a kinship relationship, mostly with grandparents. Studies have clearly shown that a kid placed with kin does better than when in foster care.

The problem with kinship care is that whereas one advantage of foster care is that the state provides a level of financial and medical support, kids in kinship care are on their own with no State or Federal financial support. HALOS to the rescue. Supported by grants and donations, HALOS offers limited financial, medical and compassionate support. It is a wonderful organization.

As I mentioned, anyone associated with the NICU must be able to cope with both sad and happy experiences.

CHAPTER 21

Opioid Babies

Opioid Babies is George's take on the medical term, Neonatal Abstinence Syndrome (NAS). The inter-web tells us the term NAS refers to babies born addicted to either drugs or alcohol. This addiction results when pregnant women are hooked on these substances. Whatever is in the Mom's body is in the baby's body. And if a baby is born addicted, the only course of action is withdrawal.

In my first several years in the NICU, I understood that most NAS babies I held were babies addicted to cocaine (crack babies). At most, I would be aware of a crack baby once or twice a month. Today, there might be as many as two or three Opioid Babies in the NICU at any given time. In fact, it is estimated that some 30,000 Opioid Babies are born in the US each year.

It is difficult for me to even try to describe the obvious suffering these babies endure during withdrawal. A partial list, from a medical journal notes 'unique high-pitched crying, jitteriness, tremors, convulsions, fever, sweating, vomiting, diarrhea, mottling, difficulty sleeping, no appetite, and dehydration'. And it seems that any NAS baby I hold experiences each and every one of these withdrawal syndromes each and every time I hold one.

One day I was holding a truly suffering Opioid Baby. The baby's nurse who was cool, calm, and collected as always, noticed I wasn't doing well at all. She pulled up a chair and sat down.

Nurse: "George, it upsets us all. You are doing everything you can. If it is too much for you, we can find another baby."

George: "No! This baby needs me. I'll hang in there." I paused, then continued, "But if this baby's mom comes in, I'm going to kick her (you know what)."

Nurse, literally sticking her finger in my face: "George, that mom is sick too."

No wonder I am in awe of the NICU nurses.

It is interesting to me that when we returned to work from the pandemic furlough in October 2020, many NAS babies seemed calmer than before. I know better than to ask, but assume new treatments and procedures are underway. In any event, it sure is better when those babies are not so upset.

The unanswered question is 'What will happen to these NAS babies when they grow-up? Will there be long-term health issues? Will the babies always have a craving for opioids? I assume these Opioid Babies will be closely monitored. We will just have to wait and see.

Enough! Enough! It's part of the job. But still, it is one more story which to me is both heart wrenching and heartwarming.

CHAPTER 22

The Kangaroo Kid

Kangaroo care is a method of holding a baby that involves skin-to-skin contact. The baby, who is typically naked except for a diaper, is placed in an upright position against a parent's, or when I do it, a surrogate parent's chest. Numerous studies, including a Cleveland Clinic article I found that helped me with this explanation, show that the skin-to-skin contact from kangarooing has a number of medical benefits which include: stabilizing the baby's heart rate, improving the baby's breathing pattern and making the breathing more regular, improving oxygen saturation levels (a sign of how well oxygen is being delivered to all of the infant's organs and tissues), gaining in sleep time, experiencing more rapid weight gain, decreased crying, and having an earlier hospital discharge. And when parents kangaroo, studies have shown a 'bonding' benefit as well. Since I am convinced I 'bond' with almost every baby I hold, I don't see a real difference. But I do know these little guys are totally and completely relaxed within five minutes of our coming together.

Kangaroo care was developed in Bogota, Colombia in the late 1970s as a response to a high death rate in preterm babies—the death rate for premature infants was approximately 70% at that time. The babies were dying of infections, respiratory problems and simply due to a lack of attention. Researchers found that babies who were held close to their mothers' bodies for large portions of the day not only survived, but thrived. And the death rates reportedly were reduced to 30%.

From time to time, I am the Kangaroo Kid in the NICU. Imagine that?

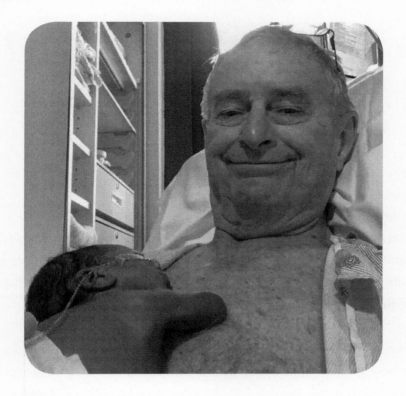

Just another NICU day!

CHAPTER 23

The No Precedents Pandemic

I write this chapter in early August 2021. The Covid pandemic is still underway, and the Delta variant has emerged. No one knows how events will ultimately unfold.

Everyone hopes the vaccines work with no delayed side-effects. Everyone hopes enough folks get vaccinated to make a real difference. And everyone hopes Covid variants which keep appearing are controllable. Time will tell.

When the Covid pandemic hit in early 2020, the new Children's Hospital had just opened. In fact, I had only completed two shifts in the new hospital when in mid-March 2020, volunteers and the volunteer management staff were furloughed. It was the longest seven months ever.

During the furlough, I volunteered to screen calls throughout South Carolina to the hospital Covid hotline. One morning a week, I worked the phones from home. My job was to chat with callers, then fill out and email a three-page questionnaire to a panel of doctors/nurses who would review the information and then make a call back within twenty-four hours. My sense was that this system worked well.

Almost everyone I spoke with was calling to find where they could get a Covid test. Most men were calling because a significant other had threatened dire consequences if they didn't get the test. One woman I spoke with was one hundred six years old and was sharp as a tack. All were frightened and worried.

The scariest call was from an upstate woman who told me she was so sick with all the classic Covid symptoms, she was unable to take my advice to "hang-up and immediately drive to the Emergency Room." I then advised her to "hang-up and call 911." She demurred, "Oh, I don't want to put them to all that trouble."

Since I already had her contact information, I told her I would call EMS for her and did so. I sent an email to my volunteer coordinator telling her what I had done and got a one-word response. 'Good!'

Seven months later, in October 2020, volunteers were de-furloughed, if there is such a word. My first day back at the new hospital was October 15. I was literally lost in the new building, but that sorted itself out soon enough.

My first couple of times back, I asked almost everyone I came into contact with, the ladies who cleaned the bathrooms to senior doctors, "Should I feel comfortable coming back before the vaccine is available?"

The answers I received were very uniform along the lines of, "Well, the first few weeks were frightening. Nobody knew what was going on. All we knew is we needed to be here, so we were. If a Covid-positive woman showed up in labor, we accepted them. Several nurses and staff did test positive and had to go into isolation. After a couple of weeks, a Covid Isolation Unit was set up, and things began to settle down. Any nurses and staff who tested positive were assigned to that unit as, supposedly, they were more immune. It is your decision whether or not to come back, but we feel pretty safe."

All this re-confirmed what I already knew—these folks are true heroes.

Another thing I realized on my return was that the brand-new hospital was also suffering from pandemic stress. 'Punch list' items which would have been promptly corrected in normal times had fallen victim to pandemic supply-chain issues. Elevators were out of service, sanitizer and soap dispensers were hanging off the walls; toilet paper holders likewise.

On my first few times back, the first thing I did was go to a nurse, ask for a roll of tape, and spend an hour taping the sanitary/soap/toilet paper dispensers back to the wall. My choice words to balky elevators had no effect. Master craftmanship, no! Fine art, no! Effective, yes!

One day, after a couple of months, I saw a maintenance worker installing new dispersers. "You will be the most popular person in the hospital," I remarked.

"These damn things have been on backorder for five months," he said. "I'm not going home until I get each and every one installed." Since then, normal new building shake-down issues are noted and, more or less, promptly fixed. The new hospital is up and running.

By late November 2020, it was clear a vaccine would soon be approved. While everyone knew hospitals would be high on the priority list to get the vaccine, the question of how the hospital would prioritize its employees remained to be answered. It quickly became a topic of conversation in the NICU.

One day as I was chatting with one of the NICU doctors about this and that, the doctor remarked, "You know, I never realized how important volunteers were, especially with the Neonatal Abstinence Syndrome (NAS) babies, until you weren't here." Note: See Chapter 21 for a discussion of NAS or Opioid Babies.

Never one to miss an opportunity, I said, "I hope they remember volunteers when they do the vaccine priority list." Our conversation then moved on to important things like how a just retired mutual friend would adjust to his new life.

That evening, I got an email with a copy of a note the doctor had sent the hospital official in charge of setting up the vaccine priority list which 'strongly' requested that volunteers not be forgotten because of their importance to the NICU team. Guess what? When the priority list came out a few days later, NICU volunteers were in the first group.

Finally, in my conversations on the vaccine with medical staff, I was surprised at how many were deferring getting the vaccine. Reponses when

I asked, 'Why?' basically boiled down to, "Look, there is good reason why vaccine trials run for a couple of years. Sure, every computer model of every new vaccine is perfect when that vaccine goes into the trial. But nobody really knows how many trials are abandoned when unexpected complications or unwanted side-effects pop-up at any point in the two-year trial. But we all know trials are abandoned with no announcement."

This is always one of those conversations when the speaker is glancing round to be sure no one is overhearing. "So, I'm going to wait as long as possible. If and when they tell me to get the shot or look for another job, I'll make my final decision."

As a follow-up, I note an article in our local newspaper that the hospital where I volunteer is one of two South Carolina hospitals which require medical staff to be vaccinated. The article also notes that some 3,000 of 17,000 hospital employees where I volunteer have furnished either a doctor's note or a "note attesting that their religious beliefs precluded them from getting a shot." The hospital also confirmed that five employees "were fired for non-compliance".

The pandemic is still playing-out.

CHAPTER 24

Answered Prayers

I have learned it is not totally unusual when a premature baby is born and not all systems are in sync. Experience has shown that when this happens and there are no other identifiable issues, it is best to wait and see. More often than not, in a couple of days, systems will come on-line on their own accord. But just to be safe, these babies often end up in the NICU.

One of the most frequent issues I see in the NICU is with the digestive track. Normally, when a baby is born and is put onto breast or bottle, the brain sends out an all systems go signal. The baby begins to suck and swallow, the milk hits the stomach, passes through the digestive system, and what's left comes out the other end.

But apparently, this signal must be triggered in the brain in the first twenty-four to thirty-six hours of life. In those rare cases where it is not possible to put the baby on breast or bottle for whatever medical reason, the part of the brain that sends the all systems go signal can go dormant. Until recently, that child would have had to wait until it could understand verbal instructions on how to chew and swallow. In those two or so years, the only option is a 'G-tube'. Yuk!

But in the last couple years, a promising experiment has occurred. I will be holding a baby with this issue and a team will come in to attach nodes to the baby's head and send mild electrical pulses to that part of the brain. Hopefully, the dormant part will wake up and send the let's eat signal.

Naturally, whenever this happens to a baby I am holding, I begin to ask questions. I was referred to a website for more information which revealed positive preliminary results. There is still lots of follow-up and additional testing to be done, but this is pretty amazing stuff to me.

Answered prayer? You bet.

Another digestive systems issue is that even when a baby can suck and swallow, once the milk hits the stomach, it is just as likely it will come back up as it will pass into the intestines. Whenever a nurse hands me a baby like this, they will clearly say, "George, don't freak out, but this baby will spit-up. Here is a wash cloth."

I call these babies 'projectilers'. When it does happen, I think it scares the baby more than me. I just comfort the baby, something like, "Hey, little brother/sister, no big deal. Let's get you cleaned up. You're going to be fine." Most of the time, the baby calms down quickly.

One day, I was holding such a baby. The nurse had given me fair warning. Everything was peaceful and calm. Then, without warning, that baby unleashed the loudest, juiciest, most explosive gas and bowel movement in NICU history. Parents and nurses three beds away were startled. My baby's nurse, only feet away, rushed over. "What happened? What happened?" she exclaimed.

As I handed the baby back to her, I said, "I think we have just heard an answered prayer." The baby slept through the whole thing. Three days later when I checked back in, that baby had gone home.

Just another NICU day!

Another story.

I was holding a baby. I had no details except the baby had been in the NICU for a while and there was frustration all around. A few minutes later, Mom showed up and was expressing her frustration to me.

At that moment, the baby's nurse rushed over. "All the tests are in the normal range!" she exclaimed with a huge smile. "Totally unexpected, so we are running them again. But you might be going home today; tomorrow for sure."

Answered prayer?

Finally, whenever a long-term baby does go home, all the nurses and staff who have worked with that baby and who can break free for a couple of minutes come together for a proper send-off as the baby and parents leave the NICU, hopefully forever.

Here is a not very good photo of such an event. This little guy had been around over a year. Somebody found the theme song from the movie *Rocky* to play as the baby and family walked out of the unit, hopefully for the last time.

Lots of smiles, and some tears of happiness.

CHAPTER 25

Then There Was Timmy

I only sat with Timmy one time. Still, his story always comes to mind when I think about volunteering at the hospital.

One afternoon a couple of months after I had moved on from the Oncology Unit, I got a phone call. "George, this is Sarah from the Oncology Unit. There is a patient in another unit who needs someone with him. Can you please come down and help out?"

In my sixteen years of volunteering, I have gotten a few, 'George, if you want to say good-bye to the baby you have been holding, you should come down now,' calls. On those few occasions, I have declined as I feel I say good-bye to every baby I hold whenever I put them down. This is more a reflection on me, an old-timer who lives his life one half-day at a time, than on what may or may not happen with the baby I had been holding.

And for another spiritual story, the one and only deal I have ever asked from my Creator is when it is time to bring a baby home, all I ask is in that nanosecond when the baby leaves this life, they will be swept into my mother's arms where that child will know true love.

But the call to come be with Timmy was the first and the only such call I have received like this. I got contact information, and off I went. This felt like an off-the-books visit, so I didn't bother to sign in at the volunteer office, figuring if I was never officially there...

At the unit, I learned that Timmy was a little boy whose orders had been revised to say, 'No treatment plan. Keep as comfortable as possible.' In other words, there was nothing more to be done.

The immediate issue was Mom. She refused to leave her son alone, even though she desperately needed to get out and begin the painful process of doing things that had to be done: arranging Hospice for the final few days, contacting her church to plan a funeral, contacting relatives and friends, and of course, beginning the unending paperwork.

I went into the room expecting to see a totally distraught and defeated Mom. But no; she was composed and seemingly serene. Once I assured her I would not leave until she returned, she began to gather papers and prepare to leave.

I looked at the bed—a seemingly sleeping, maybe, five-year old little boy.

"What's his name?" I asked.

"Timmy. He loves it if you can read to him. The nurses and I are convinced he can hear what's going on."

"I'm a storyteller," I said. "What does Timmy like?"

"Baseball! He loves anything and everything about baseball."

"Timmy and I will get along great. I am the ultimate baseball guy. Now, you go do what you have to do. Timmy and I will be talking baseball until you get back."

"It will just be a couple of hours," she said, and was out the door.

I pulled up a chair, took Timmy's hand, introduced myself, and began a story. As always, I had no clue how the story would unfold. In this baseball story, Timmy, my main character and a pitcher in the Minor Leagues, has just been called-up to the Big Leagues, to the Chicago Cubs, to be precise. Even better, Timmy's best friend George, Timmy's catcher since Little League, has been called up with him. You didn't think I would leave myself out of this story, did you? Every hero needs a sidekick. The boys are thrilled, and their adventure begins.

One hour passes, then two. Timmy and George get to Chicago, they find the ball park, sacred Wrigley Field. They learn about the ivy-covered outfield walls. They marvel over the manicured playing field and their new uniforms. They meet the players and the manager. They take batting practice. Finally, the game begins. Will they get into the game? The story unfolds.

Nurses and therapists were coming in and out of the room, doing this and that.

I story on.

A third hour passed. Can you believe both Timmy and George get into the game and do well? Absolutely, if I am telling the story.

A fourth hour passes; the story continues. The game is over. A grizzled veteran offers them a ride to their hotel. While waiting in the parking lot, guess what? Timmy meets this really cute girl who, as it turns out, happens to be the manager's daughter. George is disgusted; he wants to talk baseball. The boys celebrate their first day in the Big Leagues by having dinner at MacDonald's.

The real Timmy never moves, but I do believe he squeezes my hand every now and then, especially when baseball Timmy does something exciting. Nurses come in and out. The story never ends. Could it be the seemingly nice man who came over and congratulated the boys in McDonald's actually offered them a bribe? Should the boys report this? If so, to who? Timmy uses that opportunity to call the manager's daughter. George is disgusted. On and on the story unfolds.

Finally, five and a half hours later, Mom returns, completely flustered and apologetic. I let her know Timmy and I are now best friends forever as we have just finished our first day with the Chicago Cubs. This brings a blank look. I wish Mom well and walk out to the Nurses' Station where a crowd awaits.

"What happens with Timmy and George?" they demand. "That's why we took turns coming in and out of the room. We wanted to know what was happening with Timmy and George."

"How should I know? I replied. "I was winging it the whole way. I just hope Timmy doesn't fall for that yucky girl. That would ruin everything." This, of, course, brought on a chorus of laughter. "One of the nurses commented, "You should write a book."

Sadly, a couple days later, one of the nurses called to let me know Timmy had passed and gave me information on the funeral.

I went, and I can honestly say it was an experience unlike anything I had ever seen.

After the service, I introduced myself to the minister. As we watched the procession to the cemetery form, I told him of my experience with Timmy. "My first black funeral," I said (I was the only non-black there.) I continued. "I'm an Episcopalian. I assume you know we are known as the 'frozen chosen'. I can tell you that without a doubt, I saw and felt more pure emotion and passion in your two-hour service than I have experienced in a lifetime as an Episcopalian."

He smiled and said, "That's what we do. Come back anytime when it's not a sad occasion to see me in real action." He paused, then continued. "Timmy's mom told me about you. Come on. She's in that first car, and I know she would appreciate your saying hello."

So, we walked over. I said hello to Mom. She may or may not have recognized me. The minister got into the car. The procession pulled out. I went home and began what turned out to be an 80,000-word unpublished manuscript, *Timmy and George Hit the Bigs*. Stay tuned!

Spoiler alert: Timmy and the manager's daughter, Jennifer, do get together. Jennifer, not a yucky girl at all, plays a huge role as Timmy's and George's story unfolds.

CHAPTER 26

Final Words

Lucretia says my final words when I depart this life will be, "Who's going to hold the babies?"

And a final story.

I got to the hospital, signed in, and headed to the NICU. I found a baby I had held before. As the nurse was handing me the baby, she remarked, "This baby spits up so here is a wash cloth."

This led me to tell her about this book and the baby spit-up story in the Answered Prayers chapter.

The nurse, let's call her Nicky, then related her story. "I was one of those babies," she said. "I was in the NICU, and as it turned out, I had that problem until I was twenty-seven years old. Finally, finally, they figured it out. Something with a gland that would go crazy. They took the gland out, I take a pill a day, and everything is okay."

End of story, right? Not exactly. Nicky continued. "By that time, I had my college degree and was an engineer at a local production plant. It was an okay job, I was making good money, but, but..." she trailed off, then continued. "I realized I was always volunteering to be on emergency medical response teams and stuff like that."

At that moment, her beeper went off. "My other baby needs me, but I'll be back with the rest of my story," she said and walked out. A few minutes later she returned and continued where she had left off. "So, I decided to go to nursing school. I went part time. It took me five years. But here I am. Couldn't be happier."

She looked at the baby I was holding who was fast asleep. "Good!" she said and walked out of the room.

AUTHOR'S NOTE

Deepest appreciation to the Children's Hospital family who encouraged, and cautioned, me in both writing and developing marketing strategies for this book. Even though I may not have always taken your advice and guidance, I was listening carefully. And while herein are my views, my understandings, and my 'takes' on what I have seen and learned, I do apologize for any errors.

Sincere thanks to David Edmonds, B. Clement Williams, Russell Horres, and my wonderful proof-reader/editor Kit Alford for 'hanging in' with me through this journey.

And of course, my eternal love and gratitude to my wife Lucretia, and daughters Elizabeth and Susan for—well, for always being there when I need them.

And thanks to all who bought this book. I hope you enjoyed it and have recommended it to others. Your donations to the MUSC Children's Hospital through the purchase of this book, or through your direct donations to a children's hospital near you will make a huge positive difference.

For more information on donations to the MUSC Children's Hospital, please check out https://giving.musc.edu/foundation. If you are led to make additional donations, please note 'Baby Whisperer Fund' on the form.

For those outside the Charleston area, there are over three hundred and fifty children's hospitals across the US. Please consider them in your giving plan.